Greece & Rome

NEW SURVEYS IN THE CLASSICS No. 50

JOSEPHUS

BY
JONATHAN DAVIES

Published for the Classical Association
CAMBRIDGE UNIVERSITY PRESS
2025

CAMBRIDGE UNIVERSITY PRESS
Shaftesbury Road, Cambridge CB2 8EA, United Kingdom
One Liberty Plaza, 20th Floor, New York, NY 10006, USA
477 Williamstown Road, Port Melbourne, VIC 3207, Australia
314–321, 3rd Floor, Plot 3, Splendor Forum, Jasola District Centre, New Delhi – 110025, India
103 Penang Road, #05–06/07, Visioncrest Commercial, Singapore 238467

www.cambridge.org
Information on this title: www.cambridge.org/9781009651912

© The Classical Association 2025
This publication is copyright. Subject to statutory exception
and to the provisions of relevant collective licensing agreements,
no reproduction of any part may take place without the written
permission of Cambridge University Press

Printed in Great Britain by Henry Ling Limited, The Dorset Press, Dorchester, DT1 1HD

A catalogue record for this publication is available from the British Library

ISBN 9781009651912.

Cambridge University Press has no responsibility for the persistence or accuracy of URLs for external or third-party websites referred to in this publication, and does not guarantee that any content on such websites is, or will remain, accurate or appropriate.
For EU product safety concerns, contact us at Calle de José Abascal, 56, 1°, 28003 Madrid, Spain, or email eugpsr@cambridge.org.

CONTENTS

	Acknowledgements and Dedication	v
	Translations and Abbreviations	vii
	Maps	ix
I	From Jerusalem to Rome: Situating Josephus	1
II	A Sword in Heaven: The *Jewish War*	26
III	History Repeating: The *Jewish Antiquities*	52
IV	History in Microcosm: The *Life of Josephus*	72
V	Talking Back: *Against Apion*	85
VI	Josephan Afterlives	99
	Recommended Reading	120
	Bibliography	123
	Index	141

ACKNOWLEDGEMENTS AND DEDICATION

I am grateful to the editors of the *New Surveys* series, Prof. Phillip Horky and Dr John Taylor, for the opportunity to write for the series and for their guidance during the publication process. I am grateful to Jamie McIntyre and Melanie Howe at Cambridge University Press, and Clare Roberts at the Classical Association, for essential assistance with publication. Hester Higton's meticulous copyediting saved me from a multitude of errors of formatting and expression.

Prof. Martin Goodman generously read a draft of the whole work and offered many beneficial suggestions and pointers throughout. I am also grateful to Bunny Waring, who read over Chapter 4 and offered me her insights. My colleagues at Newcastle University ensured that I had a highly congenial working environment, particularly Prof. Federico Santangelo, *optimus princeps*. The staff at the Philip Robinson Library in Newcastle and the Bill Bryson Library in Durham were unfailingly helpful and accommodating. Naomi Alderman took the time to respond to my queries about *The Liars' Gospel*. Copenhagen University provided an excellent base for the final stages of revision, and I am grateful to my colleagues there, particularly Anders Holm Rasmussen, as well as Jesper Majbom Madsen at the University of Southern Denmark. All errors and shortcomings are my own.

In writing this book, I aimed to create something which I would have found useful as a student just beginning my (still unfulfilled) quest to make sense of this author. It is, therefore, appropriate that I dedicate it to three exemplary educators without whom it could not have been written: Val Carter, Prof. Martin Goodman, and the late Dr Simon Price.

TRANSLATIONS AND ABBREVIATIONS

Translations are my own, unless otherwise indicated in a footnote. Abbreviations for **works of Josephus** are as follows:

AJ	*Jewish Antiquities*
BJ	*Jewish War*
C.Ap	*Against Apion*
V	*Life of Josephus*

Abbreviations for **biblical books (Old and New Testament), parabiblical texts, and rabbinic literature** follow the conventions of the Society for Biblical Literature (SBL), as laid out in B. Collins 2014.

Abbreviations for **classical authors and texts** follow the conventions of the *Oxford Classical Dictionary*, with the exception of the works of Philo of Alexandria, for which the more comprehensive SBL listings are used.

Abbreviations for **academic journals** use the conventions of *L'Année Philologique*.

MAPS

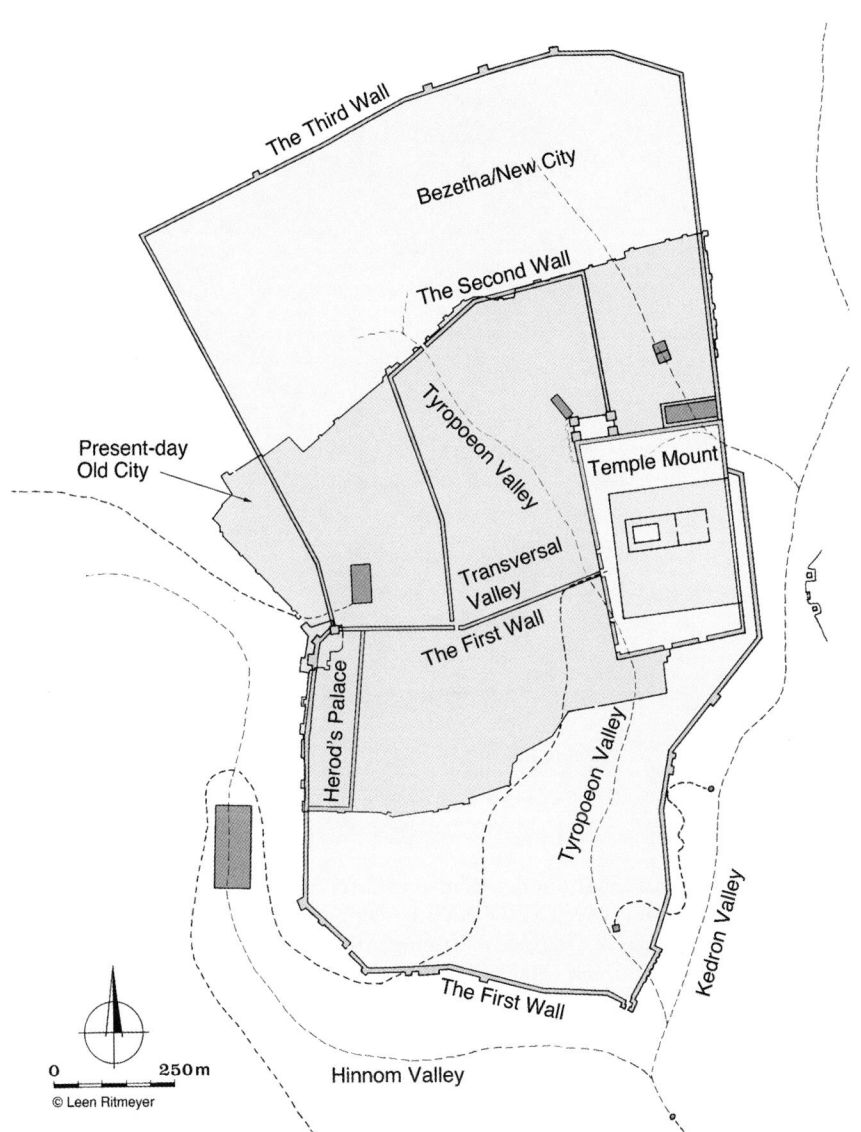

Map 1. The city of Jerusalem, 66 CE. Image © Leen Ritmeyer, used with permission.

Map 2. The Southern Levant under Roman rule. Topographic map basis: Wikimedia Commons, Erik Gaba, licence CC BY-SA 3.0 / template mapping: from Aryeh Kasher, *Jews and Hellenistic Cities in Eretz-Israel* (Tübingen 1990) p. 47, with additions by Steve Mason / mapping: Suzana Matešić, DLK / graphic: Nina Hardwig, HUND B. communication.

I FROM JERUSALEM TO ROME: SITUATING JOSEPHUS

Introduction

The Roman world of the first century CE was a world of tremendous cultural complexity. Rome's empire was an intricate mosaic of languages, religious practices, customs, and ethnic identities, bound together in a common political structure and, particularly among provincial elites, by common intellectual and cultural trajectories, which were always, nonetheless, inflected and transformed by manifestations of localism. Amid all this diversity, the subject peoples of the Roman Empire, whether western or eastern, came to be subjected to ethnographic curiosity, sometimes by Roman authors and sometimes by Greek scholars whose culture was prized and promoted by Roman power. However, not all of the 'barbarian' subjects of empire were content passively to be scrutinized. Some of them tried to tell their own, and their own people's, stories in their own words, in Greek-language texts addressed to the wider world, and to make a place for their subaltern perspectives in the dominant scholarly and literary culture of the age. In other words, some of them wrote back.

Of the ancient non-Greek and non-Roman authors who tried to tell their people's stories in this way, the first-century CE Jewish historian Flavius Josephus was among the most prolific and significant. But this statement raises a question: is it right to consider Josephus as 'non-Greek and non-Roman'? His identity is more complex than the typical presentation of him as a 'Jewish historian' might suggest. Josephus was a Jewish priest, a Greek historian, and a Roman citizen, a fine instantiation of the complex identities which were fostered by Rome's empire. Such an accumulation of identities gave him a perspective distinct from authors who can more straightforwardly be categorized as 'Greek' or 'Roman'. But is it not likely, at the same time, that it gave him a perspective significantly distinct from many 'Jewish' thinkers too? Josephus was a product of empire, with all the complexities and ambivalences that that entails.

Such a rich perspective should, of course, make Josephus profoundly interesting to scholars of the Roman world, especially in an age when the imperative to decolonize the fields of Roman history and classical literature is often voiced. But that does not seem to be the case. Although scholars of the New Testament and of Jewish Studies eagerly engage with this author's works, recognizing the value that he brings to their disciplines, it hardly seems as though Roman historians or classical historiographers are beating a path to his door. This book is an attempt to help remedy that state of affairs. While I hope that readers from a range of disciplinary backgrounds will find value in its pages, it is written very much with the Roman historian or the classicist in mind. Its goal is to provide a usable and concise introduction to Josephus for students or scholars of classics and Roman history who have not already been introduced to the mysteries, delights, and frustrations which he can present to modern readers. But it also has a persuasive agenda. This book is one Roman historian's attempt to persuade students in classics departments (and their instructors) of the value of this author, and to help them see that he deserves more of their time and attention than he presently receives.

The structure of the book is very straightforward, and is designed to be maximally useful to the Josephan neophyte. The focus will be (as it should be) on the texts: Chapters 2–5 will each discuss one of the four extant works of Josephus: in order of production, the *Jewish War*, the *Jewish Antiquities*, the *Life of Josephus*, and the *Against Apion*. Chapter 6 will survey the reception of these works, an area of rapidly growing scholarly output at the time of writing, before concluding with some general observations. But first, in this chapter, I will aim efficiently to establish some essential context, focusing on what is known of Josephus' life, of the society which produced him, and of the understandings of Jewish history which prevailed among both Jews and Gentiles in his lifetime.

From Jerusalem to Rome: the life of Josephus

By the standards of ancient authors, the life of Josephus is extensively documented, but there is a significant caveat: most information about him comes from his own works. This can raise questions about the reliability of the information presented; it also makes it misleading to use information about Josephus' life as 'context' for the written works, given that those works are the source of that supposedly contextual information. Nevertheless, in this introductory chapter it would not be out of place to survey the information which Josephus presents about himself, always bearing in mind that self-positioning and self-apologia are significant objectives throughout the Josephan corpus.

Josephus tells us that he was born in the first year of the reign of Caligula (37–8 CE). His father was named Mattathias, as was his brother; his mother's name is not recorded. On his father's side, he was a priest; on his mother's side, he claimed to be descended from the Hasmonaean dynasty which had ruled Judaea in the second and first centuries BCE (*V* 1–8). He clearly sets out to depict his family as elite and, while bearing in mind the caveats about self-promotion in his works, he is probably correct to do so. Although he was not a member of one of the high priestly families which dominated Jerusalem politics under Rome, Josephus' appointment to a significant command by a rebel faction dominated by the high priestly elite probably indicates that he was well known to them, suggesting that he and his family were among the wealthy Jerusalemite priests who moved in the orbit of those clans. In his youth (as will soon be discussed), he travelled to Rome as part of a Judaean embassy to the emperor Nero; in the Roman Empire more broadly, such a role would typically be played by members of local elites. In the Roman Near East, Greek education was a common marker of elite status, and all of Josephus' extant works indicate extensive familiarity with the Greek canon. Indeed, some measure of Greek education in his youth would seem to have been a necessary precondition for his fulfilment of that role as envoy to Nero. This, then, is probably the best reconstruction of the youth of Josephus according to the information which he presents: a privileged upbringing in an elite Jerusalem priestly family close to the high priests, and a mixed Jewish–Greek education befitting his status as both a guardian of Temple traditions and a local leader in the age of Rome.

Josephus thus probably spent much of his youth in Jerusalem, the ancient cult centre of the majority of the Judaean population. Estimates of the size of the city in the first century have varied widely, ranging from a minimal reconstruction of around 20,000 all the way up to somewhere in the vicinity of 100,000.[1] However large it may have

---

[1] For the minimalist view, see Geva 2014: 144–8; for a population of 100,000, see Reinhardt 1995: 243–5.

been, it was clearly known far and wide: Pliny the Elder calls it 'by far the most famous of the cities of the east', and Tacitus 'a renowned city'.[2] Defended by three circuits of massive masonry walls and fiercely protected by its location, Jerusalem was dominated, literally and figuratively, by its great Temple, an especially imposing edifice after King Herod's extensive rebuild and expansion in the late first century BCE (see Map 1). Situated on Temple Mount, bordered to the east by the Kedron Valley with its impressive Hellenistic-style tombs and to the west by the Tyropoeon Valley which ran through the centre of the city, the Temple was of vital importance to Judaism globally, as the only site at which cult worship of Yahweh was permitted by the Hebrew Bible. Around the Temple, in the valleys and on the lower ground roughly where the Muslim Quarter and the eastern parts of the Jewish Quarter are today, extended the area known as the Lower City. Atop the hill on the western side of the Tyropoeon Valley, extending as far as the present-day Jaffa Gate, was the Upper City, which included the palace of the Herodian kings.[3] North of this lay Bezetha, or the 'New City', a substantial suburb constructed by Herod.

Some insights into the kind of life Josephus led are perhaps provided by the excavated elite houses of the Herodian Quarter in Jerusalem, in the old Upper City, which were once owned by leading priestly families before their destruction in 70 CE. These spacious residences are richly adorned with Roman-style frescoes and mosaics, comparable in many ways to those found at Pompeii, destroyed just nine years later. However, the decorations are not comparable in every respect. Representations of human forms are entirely missing from paintings and mosaics alike, as is statuary, in keeping with the biblical prohibition on graven images; meanwhile, the use of stone tableware (considered more ritually pure than ceramics) and the prevalence of *mikva'ot* (Jewish ritual baths) suggest an appropriately priestly concern for ritual purity. This may well have been the sort of milieu in which young Josephus was raised, combining clear reverence for local ancestral tradition with a cosmopolitan openness to Roman modernity.[4]

When discussing his upbringing, Josephus emphasizes the Jewish elements of his education. Early in his autobiography he depicts his

---

[2] Plin. *HN* 5.70; Tac. *Hist.* 5.2.
[3] On Jerusalem in the first century, see Magness 2012: 133–69; Josephus' lengthy description of the city and Temple is at *BJ* 5.136–247.
[4] On the Herodian Quarter houses, see Avigad 1983: 120–39; Magness 2012: 143–6.

teenage self, like the young Jesus in Luke's Gospel (2:41–52), astonishing the learned elder priests with his insights into Torah (*V* 9). He goes on to recount how, around the age of sixteen, he undertook a course of study with each of what he presents as the three legitimate schools of Judaism at the time: the Pharisees, the Sadducees, and the Essenes. He supposedly rounded off this tour of the sects with three years spent living with an ascetic wilderness hermit called Bannus (*V* 10–12).[5] These claims are probably exaggerated (it is difficult to fit such an extensive period of religious study into his known biography), and the exaggerations were perhaps made in order to inflate Josephus' expertise in the eyes of his readers. However, it was clearly important to him to emphasize that he had received a firm grounding in the religious traditions of his people.

His earliest-known contribution to public life was the aforementioned embassy to Nero in the mid-60s CE. He went to argue, before the emperor, for the release of certain Jerusalem priests detained on false charges of sedition. He does not dwell on the impact that his first (known) visit to the imperial metropolis, his future home city, had on him, but his account of how he succeeded in securing the embassy's objective is very interesting. He claims that he befriended a Jewish actor who was an imperial favourite, that through him he got to know Nero's wife Poppaea, and that she secured the release of the priests (*V* 16). As Steve Mason has noted, such a narrative would probably have seemed entirely plausible to a Roman reader versed in hostile Flavian-era representations of Nero's reign. Nero was often posthumously depicted as an emperor shamefully in thrall to the wrong kinds of people, and so this tale fits comfortably with the way the emperor was remembered. The story highlights the canniness and political acumen of the young envoy, who arrives in Rome and is immediately able to assess the nature of Nero's regime. This is a situation in which the usual channels do not work. Josephus correctly and astutely understands that, in order to move Nero, he will need to approach him through the kinds of intermediaries who should, according to traditionalist Roman thinking, be kept far from the levers of power: actors and women.[6] These qualities of craftiness, astuteness, and political skill are important components of Josephus' self-presentation throughout his corpus.

In 66, not long after his return to his homeland, revolt broke out. According to Josephus' own narrative, trouble started in Jerusalem,

---

[5] The sects are discussed at pp. 97–8 below.
[6] Mason 2005b: 99–101.

where the daily sacrifices on behalf of the emperor ceased, the Roman garrison was massacred, and the Herodian king and procurator were forced to flee the city. Later in the year, the initial Roman military response failed, and a Roman army was cut to pieces in the pass of Beth Horon while retreating from the walls of Jerusalem (*BJ* 2.293–561). After that great initial victory (according to Josephus), a faction centred on the high priest Ananus ben Ananus attempted to assert control over the Revolt. Although Josephus presents them as the 'natural' leaders of a unified movement, it is clear enough from his narrative that some regional leaders did not accept their authority (e.g. *BJ* 2.585–624; *V* 62–7). This self-appointed 'rebel government' divided the region into districts and apportioned leadership over each area to one of their partisans. Josephus himself was given command of Galilee in the north. Josephus' two different accounts of his commission assign different objectives to his command: in the *War*, he is to defend his territory from the Romans (*BJ* 2.562); in the *Life*, his role is to attempt to curb the influence of local rebel elements unaffiliated with the new 'government' (*V* 28–9).[7] Either way, Josephus travelled north and busied himself quarrelling with local leaders, raising and training an army, and fortifying the hill towns of the region in preparation for the Roman re-invasion from Syria.

When that re-invasion came, it was under the command of Titus Flavius Vespasianus, an experienced senator who had distinguished himself as legionary legate in the Claudian conquest of Britain twenty years earlier, and who brought along with him his son, Titus, as commander of a legion. Josephus' first showdown with the Romans took place in the town of Jotapata, where the Romans besieged him for forty-seven days. According to the account in the *War*, this was a transformative time in his life. Throughout the siege, he had been receiving disturbing visions; with the help of certain biblical passages, he was able to interpret them as revealing important things about the future failure of the Revolt and, indeed, the destiny of the Roman Empire (*BJ* 3.351–3). He became convinced, he claims, that God wanted him to go to Vespasian as a messenger of these things; however, his fellow rebels refused to allow him to surrender. When the Romans eventually breached the walls, Josephus hid in a cave along with a group of rebels. After he failed to persuade them to surrender, they agreed on

---

[7] This (and other discrepancies between *BJ* and *V*) will be discussed in Chapter 5 below.

a grim pact: in order to avoid suicide, forbidden by Jewish law, they would draw lots, and each selected individual would kill the person who drew the next lot, until only one remained to end his own life. But providence was watching over Josephus. He found himself among the last two survivors of this pact, at which point he was able to convince his fellow that the pair of them should surrender (*BJ* 3.340–91).

Upon capture, Josephus requested an audience with Vespasian and, when it was granted, he delivered to him this astonishing prophecy (*BJ* 3.400–2):

Vespasian, you believe that you have merely taken a prisoner in Josephus, but I have come to you as a messenger of greater things. If I had not been sent to you by God, I would have fulfilled the law and died in the manner which befits a general. Will you send me to Nero? Why? The coming of Nero's successors is imminent, culminating in you. You, Vespasian, will be Caesar and emperor, you and your son here. So chain me more securely and keep me in your own custody. You, Caesar, are not only my master but also master of the land and the sea and the entire human race.

This prophecy of Vespasian's elevation was initially disregarded, and the prisoner was led off into captivity, although Josephus is keen to emphasize that it was an honoured captivity, with Vespasian and Titus solicitous to ensure that his needs were met (*BJ* 3.408).

History soon validated the prisoner's prophetic powers. Nero's death in mid-68 CE precipitated a civil war, which Vespasian entered from his Judaean command. In late December 69, Vespasian's Italian campaign (conducted by his allies while the man himself stayed in Alexandria) succeeded, the previous emperor was killed, and Vespasian was confirmed by the Senate as the new *princeps*. Before returning to Rome, however, Vespasian remembered the Jewish priest's prophecy and liberated Josephus (*BJ* 4.624–9). Josephus would spend the rest of the war with the Roman army, now under the command of Titus, assisting the younger Flavian in various ways, most visibly by declaiming speeches to the rebels before the walls of Jerusalem, urging them to lay down their arms (he details how, on one such occasion, he was struck on the head by a rock hurled by an unimpressed rebel and knocked unconscious; *BJ* 5.541).[8] He spent the six-month siege of Jerusalem in the Roman camp, and was presumably present to witness first-hand the burning of the Temple which he had once served as a

---

[8] *BJ* 5 and 6 chronicle the siege of Jerusalem: Josephus was present throughout.

priest. After the war, he travelled back to Rome with Titus, where he was granted further tokens of the new Flavian dynasty's esteem: land in Judaea, Roman citizenship, some form of financial compensation, and accommodation in Vespasian's old house (*V* 422–6). It was in this context, in Rome, as a freshly minted Roman citizen known to the imperial family itself, that Josephus embarked on his career as an author.

The earliest-known work of Josephus, which does not survive, was an Aramaic account of the Jewish Revolt, supposedly written for the benefit of an eastern provincial audience (*BJ* 1.3). Although he presents this text as a prototype of the extant Greek *Jewish War*, it is unlikely closely to resemble that text, which seems too Greek in conception and execution to be a close adaptation of an Aramaic original.[9] There followed the four Greek works which do survive. The *Jewish War*, mostly (or even entirely) completed by the end of the 70s, was a Thucydidean contemporary history of the recent revolt and the author's role in it. Completed late in the reign of Domitian, the twenty-book *Jewish Antiquities*, Josephus' most ambitious work, is a total history of the Jewish people from the creation to the author's own time. Appended to this was the *Life of Josephus*, a short autobiographical addendum. Finally, the *Against Apion* is a combative two-book treatise which argues against hostile portrayals of Judaism in the works of certain Gentile authors.

Josephus' years of living in Rome can be glimpsed only sporadically in the works that have come down to us.[10] Occasionally (when he compliments the aesthetic qualities of Augustus' great Temple of Actian Apollo on the Palatine, or mentions bronze diplomatic inscriptions deposited on the Capitol, or charts the route of the Flavian triumph through Rome) we may be able to catch fleeting visions of the author as tourist in his new hometown.[11] His Roman life does not appear to have been entirely untroubled: he mentions one incident when he was accused of supplying arms and money to Jewish agitators in Cyrene (although Vespasian and Titus dismissed the case), as well as unpopularity among his fellow Jews and criticism of his *Jewish War* on grounds of both

---

[9] Hata 1975–6; Davies 2023: 51.

[10] Hollander 2014 is a valuable, if (by its own admission) sometimes speculative, reconstruction of Josephus' Roman life. Cotton and Eck 2005 also attempts a reconstruction.

[11] See *BJ* 2.81; *AJ* 14.188; *BJ* 7.121–62.

honesty and aesthetics.¹² Some scholars believe that they can detect signs of Josephus' position declining between the *Jewish War* and the later works, on the basis that the former is dedicated to Titus while the others are all dedicated to one Epaphroditus, presented as a learned man with an interest in Judaism, and whose name suggests that he was a freed slave.¹³ Certainly, after Domitian came to power in 81 CE, Josephus lost the strong personal connection to the ruler from which he had benefited under Vespasian and Titus. However, less pessimistic explanations for this change of addressee are possible: his later works had less direct relevance to the dynasty, which alone may explain why they did not receive imperial dedications. There is no need to imagine Josephus' life in Rome after the death of Titus as lonely, embittered, and alienated.

Besides, our author always had family to fall back on. Josephus married four times over the course of his life. All that we know of his first wife is that she was in Jerusalem during the Roman siege (*BJ* 5.419). His second wife was a Jewish woman captured in the course of the war, and the marriage was arranged by Vespasian. This short-lived marriage violated the Torah prohibition on priests wedding prisoners of war, a prohibition of which Josephus was aware, as he mentions it in *Antiquities* 13.291–2. With his third wife, a Jewish woman from Alexandria, he had three sons, of whom only one, Hyrcanus, was still alive when he wrote his autobiography. Wife number four, a wealthy woman from Crete, bore two further sons, Justus and Agrippa, also known as Simonides.¹⁴ What became of those three sons, and how and when they (or indeed their father) died, are facts lost to history.

The people and the land

For all the complexities of his multifaceted identity, Josephus was strongly rooted in one particular place, Judaea under Roman rule (see Map 2). Properly speaking, the word 'Judaea' refers to a small territory surrounding the city of Jerusalem, roughly coterminous with

---

[12] See *V* 429 (cf. *BJ* 7.447–50); *V* 416; *V* 336–68; *C.Ap* 1.53–6.
[13] Cotton and Eck 2005 (with discussion of the identity of Epaphroditus at 49–52); Price 2005; Hollander 2014, esp. 242–304. For more optimistic readings, see Goodman 1994; Curran 2011. For more on the identity of Epaphroditus, see Barclay 2006: xxvi–xxviii.
[14] Josephus provides information on his family at *V* 426–7.

the biblical kingdom of Judah. However, both in antiquity and today, the word is often used more expansively than this, to denote a region which includes Judaea proper but also incorporates the regions of Samaria and Galilee to the north, extending from the Mediterranean to the Jordan, and comprising the majority of the southern Levant. Though small, it is a region of remarkable ecological variety, stretching from the strikingly verdant lands of Galilee in the north to the arid rocky desert of the south, and combining a broad, flat coastal plain with a rugged and hilly interior. The Jordan Valley marked the region's eastern extent, together with its two large bodies of water, the freshwater Sea of Galilee in the north and the extraordinary Dead Sea in the south. To the north of the land lay the ancient Phoenician cities and the vast Roman province of Syria; east across the river was the Transjordan, dominated in Josephus' time by the Decapolis, a league of Greek-style cities; south-east was the Nabataean kingdom; south-west was the province of Egypt.

In Josephus' day, the deserts south of Jerusalem were inhabited by an ethnic group known as the Idumaeans, the Arab descendants of the biblical Edomites, who had adopted Jewish religious customs in the second century BCE.[15] Meanwhile, Samaria, to the north, was home to a people who practised a variant form of Judaism, and whose most sacred site was not Jerusalem but Mount Gerizim, where they had their own temple.[16] Galilee, further north still, was a region of villages, lacking any significant cities until King Herod's son Antipas constructed two royal capitals there, Sepphoris and Tiberias, in the early first century CE.[17] Despite its lack of urbanization, Galilee seems to have been quite densely populated, such was the proliferation of villages found there in antiquity, possibly including a number of non-Jewish or mixed Jewish–Gentile settlements.[18]

Two major urban centres were of particular importance to this region in Josephus' lifetime. Jerusalem, inland where verdant north

---

[15] For the Idumaeans, see Kasher 1988; for their presentation in Josephus, see Applebaum 2009.

[16] For the Samaritans, see Mor and Reiterer 2010; for their presentation in Josephus, see Pummer 2009; Chalmers 2020.

[17] On Galilee and Antipas' impact on it, see Jensen 2010.

[18] The scholarly understanding of Galilee's cultural profile is changeable. While some works (e.g. Freyne 1980; Batey 1991) have painted a picture of a heavily Gentile-dominated Galilee, other scholars, beginning with Chancey 2002, have argued that this picture mostly derives from later evidence, and that there is very little evidence of Gentile presence in Galilee in the age of Josephus.

meets arid south, has already been described.[19] On the coast Caesarea Maritima, an ambitious construction project of Herod the Great, housed the Roman governors for most of the year. Though the city contained a large and important Jewish community, Herod had expressly designed it to be a centre for the non-Jewish population of the region, and it shows in the city's very Graeco-Roman design. Boasting an array of Roman-style public entertainment venues and a grand temple of Augustus and Roma, with cult statues modelled on those of Zeus at Olympia and Hera at Argos, the city connected Judaea to the wider Mediterranean world through its large artificial harbour, a wonder of hydraulic engineering using Roman construction techniques and materials.[20]

Not everybody who inhabited this land was Jewish, but the majority were, and that majority had clear ideas about how their ancestors came to the region. The widely accepted narrative of Jewish history in Josephus' day derived, of course, from the Hebrew Bible, the collection of sacred texts known as the Tanakh in Judaism and the Old Testament in Christianity. The biblical historical narrative was clearly established as authoritative by Josephus' time, and we have little evidence that any Jewish person in antiquity fundamentally doubted the historicity of the tale.[21] It is this narrative which gave Josephus his sense of history and which informs much of his work. A summary is therefore in order here.

According to that narrative, the Jewish people originated in Mesopotamia. Their ancestor Abraham left his birthplace, Ur of the Chaldees, and dedicated himself to the worship of a particular deity, Yahweh. His peregrinations eventually brought him to the land of Canaan, the future Judaea, which God promised to his descendants. However, in the time of Abraham's grandson Jacob and great-grandson Joseph, famine caused the family to relocate to Egypt as honoured guests of the ruler. Some generations later, the situation of the Israelites in Egypt had degenerated into brutal slavery. God therefore engineered the departure of his people from Egypt under the leadership of Moses. As the Israelites wandered the desert for forty years, God

---

[19] See above, pp. 3–4.
[20] On Caesarea, see *BJ* 1.408–15; *AJ* 15.331–41. For overviews of modern excavations, see Roller 1998: 133–44; Magness 2012: 170–82; Meyers and Chancey 2012: 62–8.
[21] Philo records the existence of certain people who treated the Hebrew Bible as pure allegory (*Migr.* 89–94), and who may not, consequently, have felt it important to hold to the literal truth of biblical narrative.

revealed his covenant to Moses, an expansive set of laws which guaranteed the special relationship between Yahweh and his people. As long as the Israelites lived in obedience to these laws, God would protect and champion them; conversely, any stiff-necked disobedience would result in the fulfilment of a gruesome litany of divine punishments, as detailed at the end of the book of Deuteronomy.

With the relationship between God and his people thus ratified, Moses died in sight of the promised land. The people came into the land under the command of Joshua and, after a brutal war against the Canaanites, they took control of it and occupied the territory promised to their ancestor Abraham. Initially ruled on tribal lines, in time the people came to desire the creation of the office of king in imitation of the surrounding nations. This is presented, in the book of 1 Samuel, as an undesirable development (imitating other nations is generally a bad idea in the Hebrew Bible). However, God reluctantly allowed the Israelites to appoint a king.[22] The history of the Israelite monarchy is related in the books of 1 and 2 Samuel and 1 and 2 Kings, a unified composition which some modern biblical scholars refer to as the Deuteronomistic History, and the Deuteronomistic History's initial scepticism about the institution of monarchy is retained throughout.[23]

The first king of the Israelites was Saul. However, Saul lost the favour of God and came to be supplanted by the complex figure of King David, whose dynasty was promised eternal rule by God; that dynasty would always be strongly associated with Israelite monarchy, and with the messianic hopes for the restoration of national sovereignty which would crystallize in later periods.[24] David was succeeded by his son Solomon, famed for his wisdom, who constructed the First Temple, but his other transgressions alienated God, who manifested his displeasure by causing the kingdom to fragment into two parts. The northern kingdom of Israel, comprising Samaria and Galilee, seceded from the southern kingdom of Judah.

---

[22] See 1 Sam 8:6–21 for this negative portrayal of the establishment of the monarchy.

[23] The notion of the Deuteronomistic History was first proposed by the biblical scholar Martin Noth (1943). It was subsequently expanded, and disputed, extensively. For an edited volume covering later refinements of and engagement with Noth's model, see Knoppers and McConville 2000. Römer 2020 has argued for the rejection of the unified authorship model, suggesting that, instead of a 'Deuteronomistic History', we should think in terms of a 'Deuteronomistic Library'.

[24] On messianism, see Fabry and Scholtissek 2002, esp. 11–56; J. Collins 2010, esp. 13–15.

The Deuteronomistic History does not remember these two kingdoms fondly: all of the kings of Israel and most of the kings of Judah are presented as wicked, often worshipping foreign deities and even, in some cases, stooping to human sacrifice.[25] As the transgressions of the kings and the people accumulated, God expressed his displeasure by bringing the Assyrians against Israel, leading to the destruction of the northern kingdom; a little later, God also punished the southern kingdom of Judah, bringing the Babylonians under Nebuchadnezzar against Jerusalem. Ignoring the admonitions of the prophet Jeremiah, the Jerusalemites resisted, and the result was the devastation of their city and the destruction of their temple, accompanied by the removal of much of the population to Babylon.

The Deuteronomistic History thus ends on a bleak note, but not entirely without hope. God's promises to Abraham, to Moses, and to David were eternal. If God had turned his wrath against his people, that could only ever be a temporary state. One day, when the people had suffered and returned to obedience, there would surely be a restoration of independence in Judaea, of the Temple, of Davidic rule, and of God's favour. Thus, even amid the ruin of the city and the Temple, hope could be found in God's unchanging covenant.[26] Josephus, who lived to witness a rerun of these events when the reconstructed Temple was destroyed by another Gentile superpower, was profoundly influenced by the Deuteronomistic History's response to this catastrophe of remote antiquity.

The hopes which the crushed Judahites may have been nursing under Babylonian rule did not take long to reach fulfilment. In the mid-sixth century BCE, the Neo-Babylonian Empire was terminated by the rise of Persian power under Cyrus. According to the biblical books, this change in the world order was good news for Judah: Cyrus issued a proclamation permitting the Judahite exiles to return to their land and rebuild their temple.[27] The reconstructed precinct, the Second Temple, was apparently somewhat underwhelming in the Persian period, and so it would remain until Herod's redevelopment five centuries later.[28] Nonetheless, its creation was a significant

---

[25] On human sacrifice, see 2 Kgs 16:3, 21:6, 23:20.

[26] This 'hopeful' reading of the Deuteronomistic History departs from Noth's pessimistic interpretation, and is associated above all with Rad 1966.

[27] The purported text of the proclamation can be read at 2 Chr 36:23 and Ezra 1:2.

[28] In a speech attributed to Herod, Josephus draws attention to the unimpressive nature of the Second Temple and its inferiority to the First Temple (*AJ* 15.385–7).

milestone in Jewish history, a recrudescence of hope after a period of suffering.[29]

For a little over a century, Judaea lived peacefully under Persian rule, and the reconstructed Temple resumed its function as the centre of the region's cultic life. Like a typical Graeco-Roman temple, its operations revolved around offering sacrifices, often animal sacrifices, on an altar situated outside the actual temple structure. However, in other respects it was peculiar. The Second Commandment prohibited the creation of a cult statue, a standard element in temples elsewhere, and the focus of the structure was, instead, the Holy of Holies, an empty room in which the presence of God was believed to reside, and into which it was strictly forbidden to trespass. The Temple was served by the priests (*kohanim*), a recognizable class within Judaean society, and a class to which Josephus belonged. Priests were divided into twenty-four *mishmarot* (literally 'watches', often translated as 'courses'), who took turns to officiate in a system of sacerdotal shiftwork. Each course would be expected to be on duty at the Temple for two weeks out of the year, in addition to the three great pilgrim festivals (Pesach, Shavuot, and Sukkot), when all courses were required to be in attendance to cater for the greatly inflated number of worshippers.[30]

The other central focus of religious life in the Second Temple era was Torah. While levels of commitment to Torah observance would vary from person to person, and while different people interpreted the laws differently, it is probably reasonable to assume that most Jewish people would have made at least some attempts to follow their understanding of the law. The sheer extent of the demands which the Hebrew Bible made on Jewish life is hard to parallel in other religious traditions in antiquity, except for those required of specially designated sacred individuals such as the *flamen Dialis* at Rome.[31] Some of those demands sharply distinguished Jews from others. Stringent Jewish dietary requirements perhaps made common Jewish–Gentile dining difficult. The insistence on the sole worship of Yahweh made participation in the religious practices of other peoples problematic to

---

[29] For Persian administration in Judaea, see Lipschits and Oeming 2006, especially the contributions by Lipschits (19–52), Kessler (91–122), and Dandamayev (373–98).
[30] The fullest account of the Temple's operations remains Sanders 1992: 129–310.
[31] For the fearsome list of taboos governing the life of the *flamen Dialis*, see Gell. *NA* 10.15.3–25.

most Jews.³² The observance of Shabbat was another highly distinctive feature of Jewish life. But as far as we can tell, the people of Judaea, with their curious temple and unusual customs, lived peacefully and unmolested in that century of Persian rule.

As the end of the fourth century BCE approached, all that would change. In a half-Greek Balkan mountain kingdom, a new world order was about to be born.

Japheth and Shem: Judaea in the Hellenistic world

In the *Jewish Antiquities*, Josephus provides a vivid account of Alexander's visit to Jerusalem (*AJ* 11.325–39). The king supposedly venerated the high priest, made sacrifices to God, and read his life as prophesied by the book of Daniel. In reality, none of this happened. Alexander did not even visit Jerusalem; these tales of a royal pilgrimage to the holy city were local Judaean legends. But the very existence of these legends, like the very existence of all the many other local legends which accrued around Alexander across west and central Asia, serves as testimony to the extraordinary impact which the king and his army would have on the territories that they conquered, as well as the powerful magnetism of Alexander's name and personality.

Once that magnetism was removed by Alexander's death in 323 BCE, there was nothing to hold his empire together. The Hellenistic kingdoms emerged from the wreckage of that short-lived entity, each ruled by the family of one of Alexander's senior commanders. Judaea initially passed into the control of the Ptolemaic kingdom, centred on Egypt. For the next century or so, it would be the object of frequent wars between the Ptolemies and their northern neighbours the Seleucids, based in Syria, and these wars would receive biblical commemoration as the conflicts between the kings of the North and South 'prophesied' in the book of Daniel (which actually reached its current form later).³³ The wars were likely disruptive, but we know of no major anti-Ptolemaic agitations in Palestine. In Judaea itself, perhaps the most significant legacy of the Ptolemies was the spread of

---

³² Not necessarily all. Czajkowski 2015 argues, on the basis of some papyri, that some Roman-period Jews were willing to engage with aspects of imperial cult when swearing oaths for legal purposes.
³³ Dan 11:1–35.

the Greek language, which came to be widely spoken in this region, not only by the elite. It joined Aramaic, which had taken root in the land during the Persian period, as a major local language.[34]

However, the major innovations of the Ptolemaic period in Jewish history happened outside Palestine. The early Ptolemaic period witnessed mass Judaean immigration into Egypt, and especially Alexandria, and Jewish settlers in that city came to enjoy an intermediate status, not possessing full citizenship but holding privileges which were not granted to the Egyptians.[35] Early Ptolemaic Alexandria was also the setting for the translation of the Torah into Greek, an event which, according to a surviving Jewish text known as the *Letter of Aristeas*, was the result of royal sponsorship, with seventy-two priestly translators being brought to Alexandria by Ptolemy II to create a version of the Jewish laws fit for the famous library. Greek versions of the Hebrew Bible were soon circulating widely, making Judaism more accessible to outsiders and serving the needs of emerging Greek-speaking Jewish communities throughout the Mediterranean.[36] At this time, Jewish communities were springing up in cities throughout the Levant, Asia Minor, Greece, and the islands, and even, by the early first century BCE, Rome. It was in the time of the Ptolemies that the foundations were laid for the Greek-speaking Mediterranean diaspora which was such an important part of the Judaism of Josephus' lifetime.[37]

Ptolemaic control over Palestine came to an end with the Seleucid conquest of the region by Antiochus III around 200 BCE, but it was the reign of Antiochus IV Epiphanes (175–164 BCE), the villain of Hannukah, which precipitated a severe rupture between the inhabitants of this region and their Macedonian rulers. Two important Jewish texts from the second century BCE relate the story of Antiochus' transgressions and the militant Judaean response, 1 and 2 Maccabees. According to these texts, problems originated among a particular class of leading Judaeans, including priests, who attempted to introduce Greek customs into Jerusalem (these people are often known nowadays as the

---

[34] On language use in Judaea, see S. Schwartz 1995; Macfarlane 1997; Rajak 2002: 46–65; Smelik 2013: 100–22.

[35] The precise status of the Jews of Alexandria in the Hellenistic and Roman periods is complex and disputed. See Blouin 2005: 36–43; Gambetti 2009: 23–76; Gruen 2015: 70–7, with references to earlier scholarship there.

[36] See Rajak 2009, esp. 24–63, 125–75.

[37] On the emergence and development of the diaspora, see Gruen 2015; Rajak 2018. Bloch 2022 is a stimulating collection of essays on Jewish diaspora experience in antiquity.

Hellenizers). Their sins are variously attested: they constructed a gymnasium; they 'made foreskins for themselves' (i.e. underwent epispasm, a cosmetic surgery procedure for foreskin restoration); they abandoned the traditional priestly duties; they developed an enthusiasm (*terribile dictu*) for wearing Greek-style hats.[38] Some years later, Antiochus mandated major changes to Jewish religious practice. Circumcision was outlawed; sacrifices to foreign deities were imposed; an altar of Olympian Zeus was erected on top of the altar at the Jerusalem Temple (Daniel's 'abomination which makes desolate'); any who refused to abide by the new dispensations were put to death.[39] The ferocity of the persecution prompted a militant response, the Maccabean Revolt, led by the priestly Hasmonaean family (Josephus' supposed maternal ancestors), who were eventually able to take advantage of ongoing Seleucid civil wars to establish an independent Judaean nation under a new, Hasmonaean, royal dynasty, ruling simultaneously as kings and high priests.

Whatever the historicity of Antiochus' persecution as related in 1 and 2 Maccabees, the presentation of these events in those texts offers insights into the intersection of Judaism and Greek culture in this period.[40] At first glance, both texts appear to validate a sharp distinction between the 'Greek' and the 'Jewish', and to represent a wholesale rejection of Hellenism on the part of Judaism. But such a reading would be misguided. Though 1 and 2 Maccabees are both hostile to the Hellenizers, they are also both clear that the Hellenizers were not the real cause of trouble: major unrest did not break out until Antiochus' ill-advised interventions. Although some aspects of 'Hellenism' may have been distasteful to some Jews, conflict between the Hellenic and the Judaic was not inevitable. Even the Hasmonaean family took Greek names, minted coins displaying Greek iconography and bearing Greek inscriptions, and constructed Greek-style mausoleums.[41] By the mid-second century BCE, Greekness was too deeply embedded, both in Judaea and in the wider eastern Mediterranean, for total rejection to be feasible. Judaea was part of a world whose political vocabulary and iconography of

---

[38] 1 Macc 1.11–15; 2 Macc 4.7–22.
[39] 1 Macc 1.41–64; 2 Macc 6.1–11; Dan 12:11.
[40] The bibliography on what actually happened in the 160s BCE is too large to cite here. Important contributions include Tcherikover 1959: 152–74; F. Millar 1978; Bickerman 1979; Honigman 2014.
[41] Gruen 1998: 1–140; Regev 2017. On mausoleums, see 1 Macc 13.27–9; Meyers and Chancey 2012: 39–42.

power was emphatically Greek, and even after their revolt the Hasmonaeans had no option but to play the game.

Alexander's conquests brought significant change to the eastern Mediterranean. The Greek language and Greek culture came to enjoy hegemonic status, privileged over other cultures as the marker of trans-local elite status. The leaders of the non-Greek peoples of West Asia came to adopt Greek culture themselves, usually in complex combination with their own ancestral ways of life. The Judaeans were no different, though their cultural 'red lines' were more numerous than those of the rest. Even after the Maccabean rising, Judaea continued to be part of a substantially Greek world. This would not change with the coming of Rome. The cultural order created by the Hellenistic kingdoms, which privileged the Greek and devalued the 'barbarian' even as Greekness came everywhere to be inflected by local cultures, would remain in place, forming the intellectual landscape in which Josephus would operate.

The ships of Kittim: the coming of Rome

Hyrcanus and Aristobulus were responsible for this suffering which befell the people of Jerusalem because of their dissension. We lost our liberty and became subjected to the Romans...and in addition the Romans extorted from us more than ten thousand talents over a short period of time. (*AJ* 14.77–8)

With this stark epitaph Josephus laments the loss of Judaean independence to Rome. He is referring to the intervention in 64 BCE of Pompey the Great into the region, the first direct Roman intrusion into Judaean affairs. Pompey was engaged in his campaign against Mithridates of Pontus. He turned to settling the affairs of Syria, and his attention was soon drawn to the Hasmonaean kingdom. On arrival, he found Judaea in tumult. Queen Salome Alexandra had recently died, appointing her son Hyrcanus to rule after her, but Hyrcanus' brother Aristobulus also pressed a claim, leading to a fraternal civil war. Pompey took Hyrcanus' side in the dispute, prompting Aristobulus' forces to seize the Temple and close the gates to the Romans. Pompey's army stormed the Temple, slaughtering defenders and priests alike, and the great man himself violated a profound Jewish taboo by entering the Holy of Holies. He did at least refrain from looting the Temple's treasures, according to Josephus (*AJ* 14.34–79; *BJ* 1.131–58). But even if Josephus is correct about Pompey leaving the treasures untouched, his desecration was severe. As episodes of 'first contact' go, this was catastrophic. In many ways, the picture would not improve in the coming decades.

With Aristobulus safely removed to Rome, Hyrcanus could continue governing the region as high priest and ethnarch, although the royal title was not permitted to him. Any poor impressions of Rome which might have been fostered by Pompey's desecration would be reinforced ten years later, when Pompey's fellow triumvir Crassus looted the Temple in order to fund his disastrous Parthian campaign (*AJ* 14.105–19; *BJ* 1.179). There soon followed the grim period of the civil wars which plagued Rome in the last years of the Republic, and distant Judaea was not spared from their ravages. A string of civil war combatants – Pompey's partisans, Caesar, Cassius, Antony – all headed east and raised money and recruits from the Levant, burdening Judaea with punitive financial levies to fund their conflicts.[42] The decisive moment, however, arrived in 40 BCE, when a Parthian invasion swept into the Roman province of Syria and Antigonus, the son of the Aristobulus whom Pompey had deprived of the kingship, was able to stage a coup and establish himself as the new ruler, with Parthian support. But Antigonus' reign was not of long duration. A certain Herod, a prominent and energetic Idumaean courtier of Hyrcanus, escaped from the usurper's clutches and fled to Rome, where, thanks to the patronage of Antony, he managed to get himself proclaimed 'king of the Jews' by the Senate (*BJ* 1.284–5):

[Octavian] called a meeting of the Senate. Messalla, along with Atratinus, brought in Herod and spoke of his father's good deeds and his own goodwill towards Rome, and simultaneously demonstrated that Antigonus was their enemy, not only because of his previous conduct but also because he had now taken power with Parthian assistance in a way which showed contempt for Rome. This caused consternation in the chamber and, when Antony stood up and argued that Herod becoming king would be advantageous to Rome in the Parthian war, the vote in favour of regime change was unanimous...Then Antony hosted a public feast to celebrate the first day of the reign of Herod.

Three years later in 37 BCE, a Roman army stormed Jerusalem once again. Antigonus was killed, and Herod was able to claim the office which the Senate had voted him to receive.[43]

---

[42] This complex period is chronicled in detail at *AJ* 14.119–326, and more concisely at *BJ* 1.180–247.
[43] The Parthian incursion and rise of Herod are narrated at *BJ* 1.248–346; *AJ* 14:330–491.

The long reign of Herod set a number of important precedents for the future of Roman-administered Judaea.[44] Unlike the Hasmonaeans, Herod was unable to hold the position of high priest due to his ancestry, and therefore he inaugurated the habit of the monarch appointing and firing the high priest, a prerogative which would later transfer to the Roman governors. His lavish building programme, both in his own kingdom and far beyond it, assisted in the dissemination of Augustan architectural messaging across West Asia.[45] Josephus accuses him of oppressive rule and intensive surveillance, and his domestic life was a terrible mess: over the course of his reign, he would end up executing his favourite wife, three of his sons, and several other relatives.[46] The dismal story of the massacre of the innocents of Bethlehem, from Matthew's Gospel (2:16–18), is probably not historical, but the very fact that such a story could circulate is perhaps illustrative of the reputation which Herod had earned, as is a tall tale concerning the end of the king's life. According to Josephus, Herod, on his deathbed, rounded up the most popular leading men from throughout Judaea and ordered that, when he died, they were all to be put to death, since he recognized that this was the only way that he could induce people to weep on the day of his demise. Luckily the monstrous scheme was overruled by his sister (*BJ* 1.659–60).

After the dismal old tyrant finally died, the Herodian family would remain important in the region until the death of the king's great-grandson, although none of Herod's successors would be able to establish such unshakeable and long-lasting authority.[47] Immediately following the king's death, his territory was divided between three of his sons; however, his principal heir, Archelaus, who governed Judaea proper as ethnarch, was found to be inadequate so, in 6 CE, he was exiled and replaced by a Roman governor. That basic division, with the Judaean heartlands run directly by Rome while outlying areas remained in the hands of members of the Herod clan, would persist up until the outbreak of revolt in 66 CE.

---

[44] On the reign of Herod, see Kasher with Witztum 2008; Richardson and Fisher 2017 (the former with caution). On Herod in Josephus, see Landau 2006; Czajkowski and Eckhardt 2021.

[45] Josephus gives a thematic survey of Herod's construction projects at *BJ* 1.401–30. For surveys of the literary and archaeological evidence, see Roller 1998; Richardson and Fisher 2017: 235–89.

[46] On surveillance and oppression, see *AJ* 15.365–9. On Herod's domestic trouble and the intrigues against him as presented by Josephus, see Bond 2012; Czajkowski 2016.

[47] On the dynasty beyond Herod himself, see Kokkinos 1998; Wilker 2007.

Judaea in this period was not a fully constituted Roman province; rather, it was a special administrative area under the overall authority of the Roman governor of Syria.[48] Josephus' account of this period makes it clear that Syrian governors were free to intervene in Judaean affairs as and when they saw fit, and that people in Judaea could appeal decisions of the local governor to him.[49] The governors sent to Judaea by Rome were of equestrian, rather than senatorial, rank, indicating their juniority. In Judaea, as elsewhere in their empire, the Romans showed a preference for entrusting some governance to local elites. In addition to the Herod family, and to their courtiers and hangers-on (the people the New Testament calls 'the Herodians'), the local dimension in Roman governance of the region was represented by the high priest and his circle. He, along with a court or council known by the Greek name of 'sanhedrin' (συνέδριον), retained some civic functions, including a judicial role. From the time of Herod on, the high priesthood tended to devolve onto members of only four families. This effectively created an elite within the priesthood, with wealthy, land-owning, Jerusalem-dwelling priestly families close to the high priestly clans coming to dominate Jerusalem, although it should be remembered that not all priests were wealthy, and the majority should not be considered part of the elite.[50] It is this class – elite priests with a political role under the Roman administration – to which Josephus belonged.

'Jewish customs are irrational and foul': Greek and Roman views of Judaism

Before turning to Josephus' works themselves, one final preliminary matter should be addressed. His works were, among other things, acts of intercultural communication: attempts to translate Judaism and Jewish history into terms comprehensible to non-Jewish readers. However, the non-Jewish readers who were among Josephus' intended audience were not blank slates. They came to those works with pre-existing knowledge of and beliefs about Jews and Judaism. If we wish to be able to understand the important intercultural elements of

---

[48] Eck 2007: 1–52 is the best current discussion of the status of Judaea between 6 and 66 CE.
[49] See, for example, *AJ* 18.85–8; *AJ* 20.182; *BJ* 2.333–41.
[50] Goodman 1987 remains an indispensable study of the elite priestly class in this period.

Josephus' works, we must first pay attention to those pre-existing notions, to what kinds of 'knowledge' about Judaism he could expect of his audience. What opportunities, and what obstacles, did Graeco-Roman preconceptions of Judaism present to authors like Josephus, who wanted to communicate knowledge about their people in a world where the prevailing mainstream intellectual traditions were produced by outsiders?[51]

Despite the Tacitus quotation in the heading of this section, not all Greek and Roman commentary on Judaism was hostile.[52] Some aspects of Judaism – namely the belief in the unitary nature of the divine, and the idea that God could not be represented by human hands – struck some Greek and Roman authors as philosophically advanced, leading to a notion, occasionally visible in the texts, that the Jews were a nation of philosophers.[53] Clearchus of Soli claims that his teacher Aristotle once met a Jewish man whose philosophical discourse showed that he had 'the soul of a Greek': Aristotle also, according to Clearchus, claimed that the Jews were descended from Indian philosophers called Calani.[54] The 'philosophical' reputation of Judaism led the philosopher Numenius of Apamea (second century CE) to declare that Plato, a well-known espouser of unitary notions of divinity, was simply 'Moses speaking Attic Greek'.[55] Strabo's account of Jewish origins is similarly admiring: he saw them as the better sort of Egyptians, who left their country under the leadership of Moses, dismayed at how debased Egyptian religion had become.[56]

In addition to these expressions of admiration for aspects of Judaism, we occasionally find a surprising degree of knowledge, sometimes accompanied by (clearly exceptional) familiarity with the Greek Bible. The Greek aesthetic treatise *On the Sublime* quotes the book of Genesis with approval.[57] Some scholars suggest that Virgil's poetry demonstrates familiarity with some parts of the Tanakh, chiefly

---

[51] M. Stern's collection of Greek and Latin authors on Jews and Judaism (1974–80) remains the most valuable resource for those exploring this topic. Important general discussions of these questions are provided by Schäfer 1997; Isaac 2004: 440–91; Bar Kokhva 2010; Gruen 2016: 313–32. On specific important authors, Bloch 2002 and Feldherr 2009a are helpful on Tacitus' Jewish excursus, and the introduction to Barclay 2006 is indispensable for the numerous Gentile authors quoted or paraphrased by Josephus in *Against Apion*.
[52] The quotation is from Tac. *Hist.* 5.5: *Iudaeorum mos absurdus sordidusque*.
[53] On the 'philosophical Jews' trope, see Gruen 2016: 133–52.
[54] *C.Ap* 1.177–81.
[55] Des Places 1973, fr. 8.
[56] Strabo 16.2.35–7.
[57] [Longinus] *Subl.* 9.9.

Isaiah.⁵⁸ The Late Republican polymath Varro and the eccentric emperor Caligula both knew the Hebrew name of God.⁵⁹ In the second century, the philosopher Celsus, most famous today as an early critic of Christianity, showed extensive familiarity with the contents of the Hebrew Bible, and was even able to quote Jewish traditions about Jesus which are also transmitted in rabbinic sources.⁶⁰ Furthermore, we know of certain non-Jewish individuals in the Roman world whom the sources label 'God-fearers': people who did not become Jewish but were nonetheless attracted to some aspects of Judaism, and who offered support to the Jewish communities in their cities.⁶¹ So, despite the general ignorance of Judaism and Jewish literary traditions, it is clear that some non-Jews held Judaism in fairly high regard, and others evinced indications of more knowledge than seems to have been the norm.

But outside these cases, in general it seems that familiarity with Judaism was a rarity. The biblical books, despite having been available for a long time in Greek, were not considered part of the essential canon of the educated person. A small number of 'facts' about Judaism were well known. The figure of Moses was famous, as was the basic story of his leading the people out of Egypt. This caused many Greek and Roman authors to hypothesize that the Jews were Egyptian by origin (and, though Josephus repeatedly takes strong exception to this claim, we ought to note that such a suggestion is not, in and of itself, pejorative). The numerous Graeco-Roman versions of the exodus story which circulated recognizably tell the same story as the Hebrew Bible, but the details are often twisted to the detriment of the Jewish people. For instance, on Tacitus' reading, the Israelites were not delivered from Egypt thanks to the protection of God, but were driven out by Pharaoh at the command of the gods of Egypt, who saw them as polluters.⁶² Thus, rather than God's chosen people, the Tacitean version reconceptualizes the Israelites as undesirable aliens, sources of contamination, and god-cursed vectors of disease. Tacitus goes on to claim that Moses devised the laws of Judaism and Jewish religious practice in conscious opposition to the religious practices of

---

⁵⁸ See, most recently, Hejduk 2018.
⁵⁹ Lydus, *Mens.* 4.53; Philo, *Legat.* 353.
⁶⁰ Alexander 2021.
⁶¹ This term, once a staple in considerations of Second Temple Judaism, has recently been contested. See Kraemer 2014 and Fredriksen 2015 for an overview of evidence and arguments.
⁶² Tac. *Hist.* 5.5.

the rest of the world, a Judeophobic twist on Herodotus' reading of the Egyptians as 'mirror-people' whose customs were the inverse of everybody else's.[63]

Certain elements of Jewish practice deriving from biblical laws attracted comment from Greek and Roman authors, with a tonal range extending from amused curiosity to outright hostility. Jewish food taboos (especially pork abstinence) were an unfailing source of amusement; sabbath observance was taken as a mark of laziness or extreme superstition; Jewish aversion to abortion and infanticide was seen as odd, as was male circumcision.[64] The Jewish aversion to idolatry clearly came to be suspected by some authors, who accused the Jews of venerating the image of an ass in Jerusalem.[65] Perhaps above all, the sense of separateness which distinctive Jewish customs created led to the very frequent charge of ἀμιξία, misanthropy towards outsiders.[66] In addition to these stereotypes, which all relate directly or indirectly to authentic features of Jewish law and practice, Jews were subjected to the kinds of generalizing negative stereotypes to which all the 'barbarian' peoples of the empire found themselves vulnerable. For instance, Cicero claims that Jews are naturally fit for slavery, while Tacitus remarks that they are especially prone to lust.[67]

Anti-Judaism in more extreme forms can also be found in the literary record. A particular vulnerability of Jewish communities in the Roman period was the charge of disloyalty, arising from the refusal of most Jews to participate directly in forms of imperial cult which were otherwise ubiquitous, and this dangerous charge could be weaponized by opponents and critics of Judaism.[68] Probably the most extreme anti-Jewish tale from Graeco-Roman antiquity is a conspiracy theory which Josephus reports from the works of Apion which claimed that, when Antiochus Epiphanes violated the Temple, he found a Greek

---

[63] Hdt. 2.35–6.

[64] All of these features receive comment from Tacitus at the beginning of *Hist.* 5. On pork abstinence, see Caligula, at Philo, *Legat.* 361–2; Juv. 6.155–60; and the mildly Judeophobic joke attributed to Augustus by Macrobius at *Sat.* 2.4.11. On sabbath observance, see Plut. *De Superst.* 169C; Agatharchides, quoted at *C.Ap* 1.209–11. On abortion and infanticide, see Hecataeus, at Diod. Sic. 40.3.8. On circumcision, see Petron. *Sat.* F50; Strabo 16.2.37.

[65] Plut. *Quaest. conv.* 670D-E; Apion quoted at *C.Ap* 2.80; Mnaseas, quoted at *C.Ap* 2.112–14.

[66] On this charge, see Mason 2019.

[67] Cic. *Prov. cons.* 10; Tac. *Hist.* 5.5. Tacitus' phrasing suggests that this accusation is targeted solely at Jewish men; however, Ovid (*Ars am.* 1.75) identifies the sabbath, 'sacred to the Syrian Jew', as an auspicious time to go looking for a female partner, perhaps indicating that the stereotype could extend to Jewish women too.

[68] E.g. Philo, *Legat.* 355, *Flacc.* 41–50; *C.Ap* 2.65–78; Tac. *Hist.* 5.5.

imprisoned inside. The Greek told him that, every year, the Jews abducted a Greek man and sacrificed him at a ceremony where they feasted on his entrails (*C.Ap* 2.89–108). This absurd yarn is shocking, but it is clearly exceptional. Apion's tall tale demonstrates that it was possible for one Greek author to conceptualize Judaism as a sinister cannibal cult, but it certainly cannot be taken as evidence that this view was widespread. It plainly was not.

So in Josephus' lifetime, aside from a small number of Gentile authors who demonstrated an unusual level of engagement, knowledge about Judaism was sparse and often of poor quality. Hostile variant versions of the Jews' own origin myth circulated; Greek and Roman authors show awareness of a handful of genuine Jewish customs, generally the most obvious and visible; and a limited repertoire of mostly hostile or mocking stereotypes about Jews was repeated endlessly from text to text. A few authors expressed admiration for the 'philosophical' qualities of Judaism; others spread malicious and dangerous conspiracy theories. Most authors fall somewhere between these extremes. But perhaps the key element is the unwillingness on the part of Greek and Roman authors to allow Jews to tell their own story. Even authors like Tacitus who specifically devote attention to Jewish history show no inclination to read Jewish texts. In the world under Rome, only Greek and Roman scholarship carried the imprimatur of empire. More than anything else, this unwillingness on the part of the intellectual mainstream to let Jews speak for themselves was the greatest obstacle which Josephus faced in trying to tell his people's story to the wider world.

II A SWORD IN HEAVEN: THE *JEWISH WAR*

Introduction

A star which resembled a broadsword hung over the city, as well as a comet which stayed there for a whole year. Before the revolt and the turmoil of war, when the people had gathered for the feast of unleavened bread on the eighth of the month Xanthicus, a light emanated from the altar and the sanctuary at the ninth hour of the night and shone so brightly for half an hour that it seemed like daytime. (*BJ* 6.289–90)

By means of these and other signs and portents, related just before his account of the destruction of the Temple, Josephus indicates both the importance of the events he is describing and the fact that the hand of a higher power was directing affairs. The passage comes from the *Jewish War*, his earliest extant work, produced (at least for the most part) less than a decade after the calamitous event which it commemorates. Despite being his earliest surviving text, it could be considered his most mature historical work: a brilliantly structured, tightly focused, and grippingly written narrative of national trauma, characterized by both Thucydidean political realism and Deuteronomistic grandeur of vision. It engages in *apologia* on several fronts: justifying Rome to the Jews, justifying Judaism to Rome, justifying the Flavians to their critics, and justifying Josephus to everybody. However, none of these apologetic tendencies impair the working out, by Josephus, of a distinctive and developed understanding of events. Despite its reputation in some quarters, the *Jewish War* is not propaganda. The vision which it articulates is always and entirely Josephus' own.

One of several reasons for this work's importance is its status as the earliest surviving Jewish response to the destruction of the Temple. In *Against Apion*, Josephus states that the *Jewish War* was presented to Vespasian and Titus, meaning that a version of the work, if not the final one, was complete by 79 CE, the year in which Vespasian died (*C.Ap* 1.50–1).[1] The date of the final part, Book 7, has been subject to significant scholarly disagreement. There is strong closure at the

---

[1] See also *V* 361.

end of Book 6, a marked change in prose style in the final book, some seeming discrepancies between details provided in Book 7 and elsewhere, and some very conspicuous flattery of Domitian, a rather marginal figure in the rest of the work. This has led some scholars to conclude that Book 7 is a later addition, appended to the rest of the work in a 'second edition' of the *Jewish War* which dates to the reign of Domitian, although others have argued against this conclusion.[2] I have stated my position on this at length elsewhere.[3] In my view, it is eminently plausible – but not provable – that Book 7 is later. Here, I will not insist on a later date, though I will mention the possibility where relevant.

The *Jewish War* is tightly focused and clearly structured. Books 1 and 2 cover the background to the Revolt, as well as its outbreak and the early stages prior to the arrival of Vespasian. After the preface, Book 1 begins with the Maccabean Revolt and offers, in the first half, a brisk account of the Hasmonaean rulers, the rise of Roman power in the region, and the establishment of Herod as king (*BJ* 1.31–363). The second half of Book 1 is devoted to a detailed account of Herod's reign, which reads like a biography inserted into a narrative history (1.364–673). After the death of the king, Book 2 begins with an overview of the succession struggles that followed (2.1–100), a very brief sketch of the period when Judaea was divided between three of Herod's sons (2.101–68), and then an account of the sixty years of procuratorial government preceding the Revolt (2.169–276). The second half of Book 2 concerns the outbreak of the Revolt itself, covering the abuses of the Roman governor Gessius Florus, the violent response in Jerusalem, and the rebel victory over a Roman army commanded by Cestius Gallus, the legate of Syria (2.277–654).

With these preliminary matters out of the way, Books 3–6 turn their attention to the Flavian campaigns against the rebels, with Books 3 and 4 concentrating on the period when Vespasian was in charge, and Books 5 and 6 chronicling Titus' command and the siege of Jerusalem itself. Book 3 concentrates mostly on Vespasian's campaigns in Galilee in 67 CE, with a particular focus on the activities of Josephus himself and the siege of Jotapata. Book 4 begins by narrating Vespasian's final battles in the north (4.1–490), before the focus shifts

---

[2] In favour of a late addition: S. Schwartz 1986; Barnes 2005; D. Schwartz 2011. Against: Brighton 2009: 33–41; Mason 2016c 14–15.
[3] Davies 2023: 61–73.

and the book becomes a study in στάσις (civil war), providing interwoven narratives of Vespasian's civil war in Italy and the spiralling conflict between the rebel groups in Jerusalem (4.491–663). At the end of Book 4, Vespasian leaves the region to take up his position as *princeps*, and Titus prepares to lead the final push against Jerusalem. Books 5 and 6 chronicle that final push, and are extremely tightly focused and very violent. They weave together narratives of Titus' progress with vivid accounts of the suffering of those within the walls, and they follow Titus' progressive capture of the city's three walls, the burning of the Temple 'against Caesar's will', and the final fall of the Upper City, the last rebel stronghold. Book 7 charts the aftermath, outlining a somewhat miscellaneous array of post-70 events which illustrate the restoration of order by the Flavian dynasty throughout the Roman world, as well as the final defeat of any remaining militant Jewish rebels.

Following the allusive authorial practices common in Graeco-Roman historiography, Josephus is very clear about his literary models and his self-positioning within the canon, right at the beginning of the preface to Book 1 (1.1–3):

> The war waged by the Jews against the Romans was not only the greatest of our time but also one of the most significant conflicts between cities or peoples of which we have reports. Some authors who were not participants in this war have cobbled together disordered assemblages of anecdotes from word of mouth and have written them up like exercises in a rhetorical school; other authors who were participants have tampered with the facts either to aggrandize the Romans or to malign the Jews, and in their writings you will find invectives alternating with panegyrics, but no respect for accuracy whatsoever. I have therefore decided to write for the subjects of the Roman Empire a Greek adaptation of a work which I had earlier written in my own language and sent to the barbarians of inland Asia. I am Josephus, son of Matthias, a man of Jewish origin, born in Jerusalem, and a priest. I fought against the Romans in person at the beginning of the war, and was a witness of what happened later.

This is a very efficient opening, which justifies the work's subject matter with regards to its importance, introduces the author and his affiliations, and even manages to incorporate some denigration of predecessors, suggesting why a new account was needed of a war which had, apparently, already been extensively chronicled.

What is most likely to have jumped out to a reader familiar with Graeco-Roman historiography, however, is the clear Thucydidean posturing: both the authorial introduction and the specific claim that this war was the among the greatest of all time are clear nods to the opening of the *History of the Peloponnesian War*.[4] Thucydides was not Josephus' only model: Polybius was important, too. There are numerous parallels between Josephus' and Polybius' lives and literary projects, parallels of which Josephus seems conscious, and he signals this affiliation in Book 3, where his description of the operations of a Roman army is clearly modelled on Polybius' presentation of the same subject.[5] Thucydides and Polybius belonged to a recognizable tradition in classical historiography, as writers of mostly contemporary histories with a strong political and military focus, and also as authors who had personal involvement in the events they describe. Such histories had a reputation for intellectual rigour and 'objectivity'; by marking his affiliation to these forerunners, Josephus is indicating what kind of history his readers can expect from him. The impression created is that what we are reading is fundamentally Thucydidean, a sober, serious-minded contemporary war monograph, a possession for all time.

One way in which Josephus sticks close to Thucydidean precedent is in his lack of transparency about his sources. Like his model (and unlike his own later practice in the *Antiquities*), Josephus has very little to say in the *War* about where his information comes from. In the preface, he insists upon the importance of experience and eyewitness testimony to accurate historiography, creating the impression that these are chiefly the sources upon which he relies (*BJ* 1.1–6).[6] Certainly some sections of the *War* are highly likely to have been substantially based on Josephus' recollections, above all Book 3, with its strong focus on his own conduct of his command in Galilee. Moreover, he had access to numerous individuals on the Roman side who were involved in events, and even to some people who had been in Jerusalem during the siege (he mentions that his parents, wife, and some friends of his were in the city).[7] However, this clearly cannot be the full story, as there are significant portions of the text where Josephus' own recollections, and those of his immediate friends or family, simply cannot have been of use to him. Most of Books 1 and 2 concern events from before he was born, and the description of the Flavian campaign in Italy in

---

[4] Thuc. 1.1–3. On Josephus and Thucydides, see Mader 2000: 56–103; Price 2011b.
[5] Polyb. 6.26–42; *BJ* 3.70–109. On Josephus and Polybius, see Cohen 1982a; Eckstein 1990; Walbank 2002.
[6] Compare with Thucydides (again) 1.22.2.
[7] *V* 419; *BJ* 5.419. See also *C.Ap* 1.49: Josephus obtained information on what happened inside the city from deserters during the war.

Book 4 would seem to be another section where personal recollection would have been of limited value.

In later works, Josephus mentions consulting the *commentarii* of Vespasian and Titus when writing the *War*: *commentarii* usually designated brief narratives of military actions written in a non-literary style.[8] It is conceivable that, despite his denigration, he may have made use of some of those pre-*Jewish War* literary accounts of the Revolt which he mentions in the preface. For the earlier material in Books 1 and 2, we can look at the sources which he used in the later *Antiquities* accounts of the same events and wonder whether he was already using these same sources for the *War*, although that is often speculative. In the *Antiquities*, when writing about the Hasmonaean and Herodian period, he clearly used 1 Maccabees, and he further cites on multiple occasions Polybius, Strabo's lost *History*, and the Syrian-Greek intellectual Nicolaus of Damascus' universal history (the last likely to have been especially useful to him for the reign of Herod, at whose court Nicolaus lived for a time).[9] Although the details are hazy, it is clear that written sources of one kind or another supplemented Josephus' own recollections and the testimony of other participants as sources for the *Jewish War*.

The road to revolt

Josephus' account of the background to the revolt in Judaea begins in the 160s BCE, with the Maccabean Revolt against Seleucid rule. At the beginning of the programmatic survey of the *Jewish War*'s contents which concludes the preface, he offers a rationale for beginning there. There would be no point, he claims, in relating the remote history of the Jews, since that is accurately related in existing Jewish texts. He had therefore decided to begin where those pre-existing records of earlier times ended (*BJ* 1.17–18). However, this explanation is not wholly satisfactory. It does not explain why any account of pre-66 CE Jewish history would be necessary in a work with the stated aims of the *Jewish War*; it also ignores the fact that a substantial period elapsed between the latest biblical narratives, which concern the Persian period, and the Maccabean Revolt.

---

[8] *V* 342; *C.Ap* 1.56. On *commentarii*, see Riggsby 2006: 131–56.
[9] For citations to these sources, see, for example, *AJ* 12.135–7 (Polybius); *AJ* 13.286–7 (Strabo); *AJ* 13.250–1 (Nicolaus). On Josephus, Nicolaus, and Herod, see Toher 1989; Teets 2013; Czajkowski and Eckhardt 2021.

Literary considerations perhaps account better for this choice of starting point. As an introduction to his narration of a major Jewish rising during a difficult period of foreign rule, Josephus directs the readers' attention to the last comparable scenario in Jewish history. But, on examination, the differences seem clearer than the similarities. The Maccabean Revolt was a glorious success from a Judaean perspective, while the Jewish Revolt was a costly and crushing failure. Indeed, everything about the earlier revolt as depicted by Josephus is the inverse of 70 CE. In the Maccabean case, a Temple violation provokes a revolt, for which the Gentile colonial power is unambiguously responsible; the Jews, with God on their side, respond violently and are gloriously successful; the climax of the event is the rededication of the Temple. Two hundred years later, a revolt which Josephus substantially blames on the Jewish rebels precedes and provokes a Temple desecration in 70; the Jews, who have lost God's favour, are comprehensively crushed; the climax of the sequence is the destruction of the Temple. The Maccabean Revolt is a mirror-inverted version of the Jewish Revolt here, and the stark differences between the episodes illustrate something fundamental to Josephus' reconstruction: that possessing the favour of God is essential for the Jewish people's success, and that losing it leads to catastrophe.[10] Beginning his narrative in this way reminds readers of something of vital importance: that, for all the mundane causes which Josephus will delineate in the ensuing narrative, underneath it all is the theological dimension, the divine providence guiding events and determining the rises and falls of nations and the successes and setbacks of the Jewish people.

Josephus' bleak introduction of Roman hegemony through the intervention of Pompey in the *Antiquities* has been quoted in the previous chapter.[11] There is no comparable lament for the death of Judaean freedom in the Pompey narrative in *War* 1; nonetheless, at several points throughout the *War*, Josephus identifies Pompey's intervention as the beginning of Judaean subservience to Rome, which is often expressed in the language of slavery (*BJ* 2.356–7; 5.396; 6.329). In the *War*, as in the *Antiquities*, Roman rule begins with a shocking transgression of Judaean customs, although Pompey's restraint in not looting the Temple's treasures and the steps which he takes to re-establish its sanctity ameliorate this somewhat (1.153).

---

[10] Davies 2013: 81–3.
[11] See above, p. 18.

Josephus' brief overview of Judaea between Pompey and Herod highlights numerous moments of tension and unrest: Gabinius' and Cassius' suppressions of multiple revolts, Crassus' looting of the Temple, Cassius' heavy burdens on the people, Antony's fierce repression of anyone who opposed his administrative arrangements (1.160–82, 218–22, 243–7). Josephus strengthens the credibility of his account by alluding to and invoking the established images of a number of these Late Republican dignitaries in Greek and Roman historiography. Crassus' looting of the Temple evokes the standard portrait of the triumvir's greed. Antony's openness to bribery and expressed enslavement to Cleopatra strongly echo the influential strand of anti-Antony messaging promulgated by Octavian's circle during the climactic civil wars of the Republic. We can see the same strategy later, in Book 2, in Caligula's mad insistence on receiving worship at the Jerusalem Temple, which echoes Roman traditions of the emperor's divine pretensions. By evoking well-worn tropes about such figures, Josephus makes his narrative more credible to Greek and Roman readers, illustrating how these people's conduct with regard to Judaea was in keeping with their general characters as widely understood at the time. All of this, plus the numerous abuses of Herod related in the latter half of Book 1, effectively creates a tense background for Josephus' depiction of the procuratorial period in the sixty years prior to the outbreak of revolt.

Some scholars read Josephus' sketch of the Roman period as a depiction of escalating tension between Romans and many of their Jewish subjects, and of steadily worsening Roman governance.[12] This does not seem, to me, to be quite right. That impression may be suggested by Josephus' depiction of the last two governors before revolt broke out, Albinus and Gessius Florus: he tells us that Albinus was a monster of corruption, but that Florus, who succeeded him, made him look like a paragon of virtue (2.271–7).[13] This certainly suggests deterioration in the quality of governance, but this is not a consistent picture throughout Josephus' account of the sixty years, which saw relatively good administrators like Festus (2.271, explicitly contrasted with the

---

[12] Rhoads 1976: 30–1; Bilde 1979; McLaren 1998: 21–47; Rogers 2021: 15–134.

[13] Florus' outrageous conduct (which Josephus claims at 2.282–3 was deliberately inflammatory, in order to provoke a war to prevent him from being prosecuted for maladministration) included failing to protect the Jews of Caesarea from Gentile aggression (2.284–92) and unleashing soldiers on civilians in a Jerusalem market when faced with protests (2.305).

wicked Albinus) and Tiberius Julius Alexander (2.220) interspersed periodically amid violent, insensitive, and corrupt thugs like Pontius Pilate (2.169–77). Nor do the numerous crises which Josephus depicts erupting in the period of Roman dominance seem to follow a clear and consistent trajectory of spiralling emergency: indeed, some of the most acute crises happened long before 66 CE, such as the multiple revolts crushed by Gabinius (1.162–78), the risings which broke out in several locations after the death of Herod and which were suppressed by Quinctilius Varus (2.35–79), Judas the Galilean's rebellion against the imposition of direct Roman governance in 6 CE (2.117–18), and the emergency surrounding Caligula's attempt to instal a statue in Jerusalem (2.184–203). Thus Josephus is not depicting a scenario of gradually escalating tension so much as one of constant tension, punctuated by periodic flashpoints of major discontent.[14] For the most part, a fragile peace is maintained; periodically, the conduct of a specific individual (Caligula, Judas the Galilean, Gessius Florus) will lead to violence or widespread protest; crisis is generally averted – until 66, when it is not.

But even with this being said, the portrait of Roman governance in *Jewish War* 2 is not, by any stretch, positive – so much so that it strikes this reader as remarkable that Josephus was ever seen as a pro-Roman propagandist. Roman abuse happens at all levels. Certainly, the procurators themselves can be guilty of astonishingly venal, brutal, and insensitive conduct, as the careers of Pilate, Albinus, and Florus amply illustrate. But common soldiers can be just as inflammatory: witness mocking legionaries indecently exposing themselves to festival crowds and provoking a riot, or burning Torah scrolls as they scour villages for bandits (2.223–31). In the case of Caligula and that notorious statue, even the emperor can be guilty of pointlessly inflaming the situation.

What seems to be at stake here is innovation. On Josephus' reckoning, there is an established system which, broadly speaking, works in Judaea. The Romans make certain reasonable concessions to their Jewish subjects which allow them to live according to their ancestral religious laws. They also provide avenues of petition and response through which the Judaean leaders can appeal any decisions of the governor with which they are unhappy, either to the Syrian legate or to the

---

[14] For a similar rejection of notions of escalating tension (although a rather more optimistic reading of the situation in general), see Goodman 2007: 317–32.

emperor. In return, the Judaeans maintain their obedience.[15] However, when this status quo is disregarded, problems flare up.[16] Thus, the innovation of raising direct taxation in Judaea proper inspires Judas' revolt, while Caligula's disregard for the tradition set by his predecessors by insisting on receiving cult worship at Jerusalem leads to widespread protests. On the other side, hard-line priests seize control of the Temple in 66 CE and discontinue offering the twice-daily sacrifices to God on behalf of the emperor (2.409–10), a key part of previously established practice which enabled the Temple to show its respect for the emperor within acceptable bounds; this, too, is a break with what has gone before and exacerbates the situation. To Josephus, Roman rule in Judaea had not been easy, but it did not need to lead to widespread revolt, so long as the status quo was maintained by both sides. Breaches of this status quo, by either Romans or Jews, lead to flashpoints and outbreaks of violence, which are usually crushed or averted until the outrageous conduct of Florus in 66 incites passions which cannot be contained.

The power and the glory: Rome and the Flavian dynasty

The latter part of the year 66 CE saw some significant successes for the Jewish rebels according to Josephus' account. Florus and the Herodian king Agrippa II were chased out of Jerusalem; the Roman garrison was isolated, besieged, and massacred; and when Cestius Gallus, legate of Syria, brought an army to Jerusalem, it failed to breach the walls and was cut to pieces as it tried to withdraw back to the province (*BJ* 2.405–653). But in 67 CE, at the very beginning of *Jewish War* 3, Fortune tilts in favour of the Romans. Nero, dismayed by (as Josephus puts it) the 'carelessness' of the previous Roman military leaders, decides to send in a new army under more competent commanders. It is at this moment that the Flavian family are introduced to the narrative, in the person of Vespasian, briefly and efficiently sketched as

---

[15] Josephus' account of outbreaks of violence between Samaritans and Galileans in the time of Cumanus (2.232–46) illustrates these mechanisms of petition and response well. Cumanus initially ignores a request for help from the region; when violence gets out of hand, he belatedly intervenes. Unhappy with the procurator's response, the Samaritans and the Judaeans send representatives to the Syrian legate, who in turn refers the situation to the emperor. On petition and response in the Roman world in general, see Hauken 1998.

[16] On Josephus' framing of this system in general, see Goodman 1987: 7–9; Sanders 1992: 35; Rajak 2002: 65–77.

a highly competent military commander with distinguished experience in Germany and Britain (3.1–8).

Josephus' presentation of this family, the ruling dynasty at the time when the *Jewish War* was composed, has underpinned one of the most damaging aspects of his reputation in modernity, the once widespread accusation that he was a 'Flavian propagandist'; more broadly, his representation of Rome's imperial claims in Judaea have led to him being characterized as a pro-Roman sycophant.[17] More recent scholarship has taken a radically different approach, at times conceptualizing Josephus as something like a dissident, filling the *Jewish War* with figured critique of Roman rule in general and of his Flavian patrons specifically.[18] Elsewhere, I have argued at length that both of these approaches are too stark, and that Josephus' engagement with Flavian and Roman power is a negotiation, taking account of Flavian and Roman interests on the one hand, while simultaneously using the Flavians to advance his own narrative agenda, which could, at times, be markedly different from imperial needs.[19] Whichever reading we prefer, however, it is clear that the way in which Josephus depicts Vespasian, Titus, and Rome more broadly has been of extraordinary importance to his modern reputation.

Vespasian mostly lives up to his strong initial billing. He is depicted throughout as a competent general, decisive in action (indeed, Josephus obscures the fact that Vespasian's Galilean campaign was rather slow and cautious).[20] He generally avoids fighting in person, although on the one occasion when he does come under personal attack, during Josephus' outstandingly vivid description of the assault on Gamala, he acquits himself creditably (4.31–5).[21] By comparison with his son, he might be said to be somewhat lacking in more humane qualities, though never to a problematic extent, and we are shown that he is capable of mercy when appropriate.[22] A more convincing criticism may be that his honesty is somewhat lacking: he mendaciously promises Josephus himself his safety when Vespasian intends to kill him upon capture, and he offers a false amnesty to the rebel defenders of

---

[17] E.g. Graetz 1888: 457–8; Schlatter 1923; Yavetz 1975; Alon 1977: 252–68; M. Stern 1987.
[18] Mason 2003a; Barclay 2005; Mason 2005a and b; Spilsbury 2005.
[19] Davies 2023.
[20] Mason 2016a: 335–401; Davies 2023: 74–84, 118–20.
[21] Davies 2023: 136–8.
[22] Davies 2023: 79–80, 134–6.

Tarichaeae before executing or enslaving them (3.346–9; 3.397; 3.532–40).[23]

Josephus is very careful when depicting Vespasian's entrance into the Roman civil war of 69 CE which elevated him to the Principate: according to the *Jewish War*, Vespasian was reluctant to declare his candidacy, only yielding after protracted resistance thanks to the coercion of his soldiers and his own patriotic concern for Rome under the tyrant Vitellius.[24] He is repeatedly shown as the recipient of the favour of God. On the one hand, this chimes nicely with Vespasian's own political messaging (he seems to have been keen to present himself as the favoured candidate of the divine); on the other hand, it reattributes responsibility for the rise of Vespasian from 'the gods' to the Jewish God, a move which the emperor may not have appreciated given the denigration of Judaism which was characteristic of Flavian self-promotion.[25] Furthermore, as Steve Mason has noted, Josephus' eagerness to credit God for Flavian success, both in the civil war and at Jerusalem, could be seen to deprive the Flavians of the glory of their own achievements and present them as little more than puppets in a divine plan.[26] Overall, Josephus' Vespasian is a fairly rounded portrait, which is broadly complimentary and sensitive to the emperor's needs (as all contemporary representations of Vespasian needed to be, given the limitations on political speech at Rome), while also allowing space for failings and shortcomings, and using Vespasian and his career to advance Josephus' own theological reading of the Revolt.

Titus is a much more commanding and charismatic presence in the *Jewish War*. Unlike his father, he leads from the front, frequently displaying reckless bravery and eagerness to be at the heart of the action. His personal battlefield interventions are often decisive, tilting the fortunes of war.[27] In addition to this outstanding physical courage, Titus' second major characteristic is his remarkable kindness: time and again, he shows compassion and clemency, often seeking to minimize losses and sparing whomever he can.[28] These central character traits of Josephus' Titus do not always suggest a positive reading. His courage can shade into recklessness, as his own officers recognize. His clemency

---

[23] Hollander 2014: 92; Mason 2016a: 123–5; Davies 2023: 138–9.
[24] Davies 2023: 98–127.
[25] Davies 2023: 84–98.
[26] Mason 2005a: 254–8.
[27] Paul 1993; Davies 2023: 146–9.
[28] Davies 2023: 150–3.

can seem like weakness or naivety, and he can, at times, appear an ineffective leader, perhaps due to his indulgence of his troops (his failure to prevent the burning of the Temple in Book 6 is the clearest example of this).[29] As Zvi Yavetz noted, this depiction of Titus' clemency seems attuned to his needs late in the reign of his father, as Suetonius informs us that, at that time, Titus suffered from a terrible reputation at Rome, in part for thuggishness.[30] But Josephus does not shy away from acknowledging the problems that this awkward combination of recklessness and kindness can present: as with Vespasian, the portrait of Titus is not uniformly positive, and is in fact rather rounded and realistic, conscious of Titus' importance and the respect which he was due as Josephus' patron, but a long way from propaganda or panegyric.

As for Rome in general, Josephus' somewhat unflattering depiction of Roman rule during the procuratorial period has already been considered. During the narrative of the Revolt, too, there seems little here in the way of propaganda. Even Rome's agents and apologists are remarkably clear-eyed about Roman rule. When urging the people to abandon rebellion in 66, King Agrippa II fully acknowledges the brutality of procuratorial government (2.352), and even compares Roman occupation to slavery (2.355–6):

Your present enthusiasm for liberty is untimely. It would have been appropriate for you to fight to preserve your freedom at an earlier stage, since slavery is a hard thing to endure and fighting to avoid it is justified. But after being subjected, those who fight to break that subjection are not lovers of liberty but disobedient slaves. The time when it would have been right to fight hard to be free of Rome was when Pompey came to our land.

The same slavery metaphor recurs in later speeches too: by Josephus at the walls of Jerusalem, urging the rebels to lay down their arms (5.395); and by Titus himself in a chillingly contemptuous oration delivered to the last remaining Jerusalem rebels after the destruction of the Temple (6.331; 6.350). As Myles Lavan has noted, the use of slavery language is common in Graeco-Roman historiographical accounts of provincial revolts, but elsewhere it is usually put in the mouths of critics of empire, not apologists.[31] In Josephus, the spokesmen of empire are honest about what Roman imperial rule is: enslavement and exploitation.

---

[29] Davies 2023: 160–8.
[30] Yavetz 1975; Suet. *Tit.* 6–7.
[31] Lavan 2014.

What is missing from all this, as Menahem Stern noted long ago, is any of the usual cant put about by proponents of Roman imperialism.[32] Here we find no paternalistic presentations of Romans as liberators or 'saviours and benefactors'; no notion that Rome rules because of the extravagant piety of the Romans; no celebration of Rome as the bringer of universal peace. Similarly, the account of the rise of Roman power over the region in Books 1 and 2 does not indulge in Livian fantasies of defensive imperialism, another ancient justification for colonialism.[33] Far from propaganda, the *Jewish War* gives us Roman imperialism in its naked form, shorn of all pretence, exposed for what it is without any of the consolations of specious *laus imperii*.

Bandits, tyrants, and 'terrorists': the opposition

Josephus' characterization of Rome is less than flattering, but the same can certainly be said for his depiction of Rome's enemy in the war, the multitude of distinct factions and movements which made up the belligerent parties of the Jewish Revolt. He sets the tone early, with an important paragraph in the Book 1 preface which establishes the terminology that he will deploy concerning these groups (1.10–11):

> Internecine conflict (στάσις) destroyed Judaea, and the Jewish tyrants (τύραννοι) are to blame for bringing fire and the unwilling hands of the Romans down upon the Temple. Titus Caesar himself is a witness of this: he destroyed the city, but all through the conflict he pitied the Jews who were oppressed by the partisans (στασιασταί). On more than one occasion he chose to postpone storming the city so that the guilty parties might repent. If any reader disapproves of my condemnations of the tyrants (τύραννοι) and their bandit forces (τὸ λῃστρικόν), or my laments for Judaea's suffering, I would ask him to forget the rules of history and indulge my emotion.

This is the lexical field to which Josephus will return repeatedly when delineating the Jewish rebels, largely regardless of their specific faction or allegiance. The term στασιασταί, participants in *stasis*, connects the *Jewish War* to one of the central concerns of his great model, Thucydides, while also illustrating Josephus' economy of blame. In Thucydides, στάσις was almost a pandemic, consuming whole communities; in Josephus, it is one particular kind of figure, the militant rebel unaffiliated with the early 'rebel government', who is consistently

---

[32] M. Stern 1987.
[33] For Roman justifications for empire, see Brunt 1979; Webster 1995.

blamed for στάσις, which is a significant marker of blame, as στάσις itself is, as we can see in the quotation above, sometimes cited as responsible for the disaster of 70 CE.³⁴

Rebel leaders are commonly labelled τύραννοι, a term which, in Greek, could denote either illegitimate leaders who acquire power extra-constitutionally or simply bad monarchs. Josephus' τύραννοι are both: people from outside the traditional leadership who become leaders of specific factions, and who proceed to rule badly and irresponsibly, primarily in their own interests, demonstrating the lack of self-control which was the hallmark of the classic tyrant in Greek literature.³⁵ Terminology connected to λῃσταί, or bandits, is also very common throughout the work, reflecting an easy association between criminality and anti-imperial activity.³⁶ One final term, which does not feature in the quoted paragraph but is also frequently applied by Josephus to these figures, is νεωτερίζοντες and related terminology, 'revolutionaries' or 'seekers after innovation'. Often a pejorative term in classical historiography, this word connects to another feature of Josephus' presentation: that rebels were more likely to be poor and young, with the qualities of youth and poverty supposedly inclining people more towards reckless innovation.³⁷ This, then, is the general picture of a militant rebel according to Josephus' presentation: most likely poor, young, engaged in criminal activities, hankering after innovation, engaging enthusiastically in ruinous στάσις, and in thrall to a demagogic and self-interested tyrant.

The details of the struggles between different rebel groups and leaders are labyrinthine, and too complex to be summarized here in anything but the broadest outline. To modern readers, these factional feuds can carry unfortunate echoes of the People's Front of Judaea and the Judaean People's Front. The first of the rebel groups to receive a name from Josephus are called zealots, which he cites as a self-designation (4.160–1):

The most highly esteemed of the high priests, Jesus ben Gamalas and Ananus ben Ananus, convened meetings and harshly condemned the people for their complacency

---

³⁴ On στάσις in Josephus, see Price 2011b; Davies 2023: 121–3.
³⁵ On Josephus' *tyrannoi*, see Rhoads 1976: 162–3. Although the word was originally non-pejorative, by the time of Josephus it had acquired thoroughly and consistently sinister connotations.
³⁶ On bandit language in Josephus, see Horsley 1979; Ben Yishai 2021.
³⁷ Mader 2000: 27–8.

and urged them to resist the 'zealots' – this was what these people called themselves, pretending that they were zealous for virtuous conduct when in fact they were zealous for the worst and most extreme of vices.

Thus, with biting irony, does Josephus explain this name to his Graeco-Roman readers. His Jewish readers would likely spot a biblical allusion here, too, as terminology related to 'zeal' (*qanah* in Hebrew, ζῆλος in Greek) was marked in Judaism in this period. These terms tended to be connected to the story of the priest Phinehas in Numbers 25, who, motivated by 'zeal', slew an Israelite man and his Midianite concubine in defence of his interpretation of Torah. Thus, the term denoted a willingness to use violence in defence of Jewish law. Josephus initially uses the word to denote a group of militant priests who seize control of the Temple; later, it comes to be extended to cover a group of Galilean rebels who have coalesced under the leadership of John of Gischala, a personal enemy of Josephus.[38]

Another important rebel category, the *sicarii*, apparently traces its origins to the reign of Nero. Their emergence is described by Josephus as follows (2.254–6):

Thus the rural districts were cleansed [of bandits], but a new kind of banditry was emerging in Jerusalem, those who were called *sicarii*, who murdered people by daylight right in the heart of the city, and who were especially active during festivals. They learned to blend in with the crowds and to conceal in their clothing small daggers with which they would murder their political opponents. When they fell down dead, the murderers acted astonished like the rest of the crowd. By behaving in this way, they remained undetected. Their first victim was the high priest Jonathan, and after his murder there were multiple killings every day.[39]

The methods of the *sicarii* as sketched here have struck some modern readers as reminiscent of modern-style terror groups, leading to a surprising amount of scholarship on them by academics who work on twentieth- and twenty-first-century terrorism.[40] Josephus does not specify whether *sicarius* was a self-chosen name or an outside label; however, the term is interesting. A Latin word which originally denoted a knifeman (appropriately enough, given the tactics elaborated by Josephus above), *sicarius* evolved to mean both a general murderer and a violent political troublemaker in an urban context (note the

---

[38] On zealots, see Donaldson 1990; Horsley and Hanson 1999: 216–43.
[39] The picture is somewhat complicated at *BJ* 7.254, where Josephus seems to indicate that the *sicarii* emerged long before this, in 6 CE.
[40] E.g. Rapoport 1983; Kaplan 2019; Rapoport 2022: 13–64.

distinction made by Josephus between the *sicarii* and the rural bandits). The *sicarii* were present in Jerusalem to assist with the early rebel movements; however, after their leaders were treacherously killed by a different rebel faction, they withdrew to Masada and spent the rest of the war sheltering there, not participating in the Jerusalem revolt.[41]

Another major element in the Jerusalem rebellion is a reminder of the importance of regionality to the politics of this period. Josephus depicts a significant contingent of Idumaeans travelling to Jerusalem to assist in the Revolt. When he introduces them, at a time when the zealots decided to summon the Idumaeans to assist them in their struggles against another faction, he characterizes them ethnographically as a typical 'barbarian' people, eager for turbulence and conflict (4.231):

> They knew that the Idumaeans would obey, because they are a turbulent and violent people, passionately enthusiastic about upheaval and always stirring up revolution. It would only take a little flattery to get them rushing to arms and charging into battle as if to a festive occasion.

These Idumaeans eventually leave Jerusalem (4.305–52), alienated from the zealots, before falling in with the final major component of the Revolt, a gang of 'bandits' under the command of Josephus' other principal 'tyrant', Simon bar Gioras.

A veteran of the battle at which Cestius Gallus had been defeated, Simon had subsequently been shut out of the leadership by the elite self-proclaimed 'rebel government' in 67.[42] After a period with the *sicarii* on Masada, Simon gathered his own gang of 'bandits' together, before uniting with the Idumaeans and heading for Jerusalem to press his own claim to leadership (4.503–13). He is characterized very differently from the other pre-eminent 'tyrant', John of Gischala. While John is a γόης, a trickster and manipulator who gets his way with stratagems (for examples, see 4.92–116, 208–24), Simon is a creature of unrestrained violence and wrath, more beast than man, as illustrated by the following episode, after the zealots have abducted his wife to use as leverage during negotiations (4.540–4):

> He advanced to the walls of Jerusalem like some wounded beast unable to catch its hunters, venting his fury on anyone he caught. Anybody who left the city looking for vegetables or timber was seized, tortured, and indiscriminately killed, including elderly and

---

[41] On the *sicarii* in Josephus, see Brighton 2009; Vandenberghe 2016.
[42] For Simon's role at Beth Horon, see *BJ* 2.517–22. For his early 'banditry' and withdrawal to Masada, see *BJ* 2.652–3.

unarmed civilians. So extreme was Simon's anger that he was ready to gnaw on their dead bodies...This behaviour terrified not only the ordinary people but even the zealots, so they sent back his wife.

These multiple factions, each characterized distinctly but all presented negatively by Josephus, jostle incessantly, murderously, and ruinously with each other in dizzying, kaleidoscopic configurations, betrayal upon betrayal and massacre upon massacre, until they reach the situation which Titus finds when he approaches the walls in 70 CE, with John and the zealots in command of the Temple and parts of the Lower City, Simon and the Idumaeans controlling the Upper City, and the *sicarii* sitting secure on their rock at Masada.

For Josephus, perhaps the most significant moment in these internecine struggles comes in Book 4, when the zealots treacherously murder Ananus ben Ananus, the head of the elite faction which appointed Josephus to his Galilean command, and which Josephus presents far more positively than any of the other groups. He affords Ananus a fulsome obituary notice, modelled in part on that which Thucydides supplies for Pericles, which concludes with personified Virtue herself lamenting the murder (4.324–5):

Only recently had these men been wearing the sacred vestments, presiding over universally renowned rites and revered by pilgrims from all over the world. Now their stripped bodies were visible, left out to feed dogs and scavengers. I can picture Virtue herself mourning these men, lamenting the fact that she had been so completely defeated by Vice.[43]

Had Ananus lived and stayed in control, Josephus opines, agreement with the Romans might still have been possible. His murder, and the removal of any reasonable leadership from the rebel side, was a clear sign that God had doomed the Temple to destruction. The parallels with the Thucydidean intertext are clear and revealing. After Pericles' death, Athenian leadership passed to inferior parties, demagogues whose poor stewardship doomed Athens to defeat. Similarly, Ananus was supplanted by demagogic τύραννοι, and the result was ruin for Jerusalem. How could it have been otherwise, Josephus suggests, with people such as these in charge?

---

[43] Cf. Thuc. 2.65.

The destruction of the Jerusalem Temple

The destruction of the Jerusalem Temple as related in Book 6 is not the end point of the *Jewish War*, yet it is, in many ways, the most significant episode in the work. At the beginning of this chapter, we saw how Josephus describes some of the portents which predicted the fall of the Temple. Throughout the work, he repeatedly stresses that God doomed the Temple, largely because of the excesses and transgressions of the rebels, and he does so both in the narrative voice and in the voices of several prominent speakers, including Titus, Eleazar ben Yair, and Josephus himself (e.g. *BJ* 5.412–14; 6.250; 6.346–7; 7.328–33). First-time readers of the *Jewish War* in Flavian Rome would, of course, have been well aware of the fate of the Temple long before reaching the relevant portion of Book 6: they lived in a city where the ruling Flavian dynasty had intensively commemorated that event in a wide range of media, usually in triumphalist terms. The Flavians, indeed, presented the fall of Jerusalem as the cornerstone of their upstart dynasty's legitimacy.[44] Thus, Josephus' first readers will have known from the outset that this was coming, and will have surely understood that it was a significant event, whether viewed from a Jewish or a Roman perspective. So, when the terrible moment arrives, how does Josephus handle the responsibility of depicting such a significant and topical event?

According to Josephus' account (*BJ* 6.220–315), the destruction of the Temple was a terrible failure of Roman command. After his army reaches the Temple's walls and sets fire to the gates into the complex, Titus holds a council of war to debate the sanctuary's future. His officers suggest several possible courses of action but Titus, in keeping with the extraordinary clemency which Josephus has stressed throughout, opts for the most merciful option possible: the Temple is to be destroyed under no circumstances, even if the Jewish rebels continue to use it as a fortress. However, this is not to be. When his soldiers breach the gates, during fighting in the courtyard a soldier hurls a firebrand into the structure and flames take hold. As the fighting intensifies, more soldiers take up the bombardment, and soon the Temple is burning. Titus rushes to the scene in person and attempts to restrain his soldiers, but they ignore his threats and commands. Admitting

---

[44] Edwards 1992; Cody 2003; Noreña 2003; Davies 2023: 104–8.

defeat, Titus briefly inspects the interior of the building before withdrawing, unwillingly giving up the Temple to its fate.

The strong stress here on Titus' innocence is clear; when combined with Josephus' long-standing reputation as a Flavian propagandist, this narrative has predictably elicited scholarly suspicion. Most of the copious scholarship which this episode has generated has been solidly historicist in orientation, focused less on Josephus' text than on 'what really happened' in 70 CE, and concerned, above all, with assessing the plausibility of Josephus' claim that Titus opposed the destruction of the Temple. Most such scholarship has concluded that Josephus is probably lying, that Titus ordered the Temple to be destroyed, and that Josephus supplied his mendacious account to burnish his patron's reputation.[45] Very few scholars have been prepared to argue that Josephus' account is probably true.[46] Such a strong consensus in favour of mendacity may seem persuasive; however, the mendacity thesis raises severe and unaddressed problems. Above all, why would a supposed pro-Flavian propaganda narrative deviate so strongly from the way in which the Flavians themselves were commemorating the event, not as a regrettable and grievous error or a failure of command but as a glorious capstone achievement of the dynasty? Only in Josephus, amid his Flavian contemporaries, do we find any sense that the destruction of the Temple is something that should be pitied or regretted. It is probably impossible to ascertain Titus' actual stance towards the fate of the Temple in 70 CE. Moreover, the question is not especially interesting. It is more productive to think less about what actually happened in 70 and more about how Josephus' contested narrative functions as literature.

Titus' attitude to the Temple and his response to its destruction can productively be seen as exemplary for readers, guiding their expected response. He admires the Temple, is eager to save it, and is saddened when he cannot. Josephus' focus on Titus' response heightens the emotionality of this narrative, something which Josephus himself underlines in a fascinating sentence back in the Book 1 preface (partially quoted earlier in this chapter; 1.9–12):

---

[45] Proponents of this position include Price 1992: 162–74; Spilsbury 2002; Barnes 2005; Pucci ben Zeev 2011.

[46] Leoni 2001; Rajak 2002: 206–12; Goodman 2007: 440–3; Leoni 2007.

I will narrate the deeds of both sides with accuracy, but I will express myself in words suitable to the events being described and to my own suffering, and I shall give myself permission to express grief at the fate that befell my country...If any reader disapproves of my condemnations of the tyrants and their bandit forces, or my laments for Judaea's suffering, I would ask him to forget the rules of history and understand my emotion. Our city was, of all the cities under Roman rule, the one to be plunged to the deepest pitch of suffering from the apex of prosperity.

Thus, Josephus is aware of the 'rules of history', but he asks the reader to excuse him, particularly concerning the destruction of the city and the Temple.[47] This reinforces Titus' grief on the ground, emphasizes the historian's own close connection to the events being described, and serves to elevate the destruction of the Temple above other episodes in the work: this sequence cannot be expected to adhere to the Thucydidean detachment which supposedly characterizes the rest of the text. In so powerfully activating the language of pity and emotionality, Josephus moves his account of the Temple's destruction into the generic field of tragedy, something also suggested by the inevitability of these events. Even Titus, for all his power, cannot avert the foreordained disaster. Josephus' narrative duly evokes pity and terror, Aristotle's two key drivers of tragedy.[48] And, in the *Jewish War*'s context of production, this was revolutionary. The Flavians celebrated the destruction of Jerusalem as a great triumph of Rome over hateful and intransigent barbarians. Josephus tries to prompt his Roman readers towards a different response, more in tune with the victims' perspective, to see the dynasty's glorious triumph as profoundly regrettable, and to lament what is lost, even in a justifiable and necessary war.

But other elements are also at play in the Temple destruction sequence. We have already intuited the hand of God behind these events from the prodigies which Josephus reports. Elsewhere, at the end of the account of the destruction, our author relates a remarkable calendrical coincidence (6.250):

Long ago, God had condemned the Temple to the flames. As the years passed, the day of its fatal reckoning had arrived, the tenth of the month Loüs, the anniversary of that historic burning of the Temple by the king of Babylon.

Josephus exploits this coincidence to prove the intentionality of history, the presence of a divine hand guiding these events. The correlation also

---

[47] On emotion, historiography and Josephus, see Glas 2020; Teets 2020; Mirguit 2022.
[48] Arist. *Poet.* 1449b.

creates a strong parallelism between the destruction of the Second Temple and the destruction of the First by Nebuchadnezzar, related at the end of the Deuteronomistic History, mourned in the book of Lamentations, and foreseen by the prophets Jeremiah and Ezekiel. And indeed, throughout the *Jewish War*, Josephus recurrently evokes these parallels, weaving a dense web of connections between the two catastrophes. He describes how the same miracle (the sudden abundance, when the conqueror approaches the city, of springs which had previously dried up for the defenders) occurs to both Titus and Nebuchadnezzar (5.409–412).[49] Josephus himself plays the role of Jeremiah, the prophet despised by his own people, who attempts in vain to urge the people to surrender to avoid disaster, when he restages Jeremiah's Temple Sermon for the rebels in the city, even comparing himself to the prophet in the middle of the speech where he assumes the prophet's role (5.391–3).[50] His description of the Temple gate miraculously opening and God departing the holy precinct ahead of the Roman siege (6.293–7) alludes to the departure of the glory of God from the Temple ahead of the Babylonian siege in the book of Ezekiel (Ezek 10).[51]

Most strikingly of all, such parallelism is strongly suggested by Josephus' grotesque narrative of the cannibalism of Maria of Bethezuba. Coming at the climax of a long description of the agonies suffered by the population of Jerusalem during the siege, Josephus relates how one woman, a wealthy refugee from Transjordan, was driven to such straits that she killed, cooked, and ate half of her own infant son (6.201–19).[52] This passage, a grisly highlight of the *Jewish War*, can and should be read in the light of biblical precedent. Among the curses which God pronounces against future disobedient Israelites at the end of Deuteronomy is the specific claim that a siege will afflict the city in which mothers will eat their own offspring (Deut 28:53–7). The books of Jeremiah and Lamentations both specifically apply this prophecy to the destruction of Jerusalem by Nebuchadnezzar (Jer 19:9; Lam 2:20, 4:10). So, once again, the two Temple destructions parallel each other, as Josephus depicts Deuteronomic curses which came to fulfilment at the destruction of the First Temple recurring in 70 CE. Some

---

[49] On this episode, see Thérond 1981: 241–3; Paul 1993; Davies 2023: 156–8.
[50] See Cohen 1982a; Ferda 2013.
[51] See Davies 2019.
[52] On Maria, see Mader 2000: 140–6; Gleason 2001; Chapman 2005: 142–5; Chapman 2007a; Mason 2016a: 116–21.

of his Babylonian parallels are transparent and explicit, perceptible even to non-Jewish readers; others are more covert, likely to be noticeable only to readers with expertise in the Hebrew Bible. But, taken together, there can be no doubt that Josephus wants his readers to understand that this is recurrent history, and that, however tragic and bleak 70 may have seemed, it was not unprecedented. This had all happened before.

This all has implications for the force of Josephus' conception. Just like the Deuteronomistic History can plant a seed of hope amid the desolation of its ending thanks to God's eternal covenant, so too Josephus is able to leaven the bleakness of *Jewish War* 6 by alluding to that precedent. He reaches back deep into Jewish history to find the tools to understand and process the calamity of 70 CE. His Jewish readers would be keenly aware that the terrible events under Nebuchadnezzar had a hopeful sequel: the Temple and city restored, the people returned. If this truly is recurrent history, and if God's covenant remains eternal, then Judaea post-70 must surely also be able to look forward to a return of God's favour. As Josephus' Jewish readers would certainly have recognized, despite the Babylonian disaster, Judaism still existed in their time, and the Neo-Babylonian Empire, Rome's analogue, did not. Josephus' insistence on reading the events of 70 in the light of this remote-past history must surely have raised hopes, and questions, and those questions concerned not only the implied future of Judaism but also the implied future of Rome.

Happily ever after?

Book 7, which concludes the work, thus picks up amid devastation, with the Temple destroyed, the Upper City taken, and the villainous tyrants Simon and John both apprehended amid the ruins. The concluding book has puzzling moments: the very tight focus of the preceding work, especially Books 5 and 6, breaks down, and numerous episodes with no close connection to the Revolt or even Jewish history are included. However, its basic structure is clear enough: the first major section concerns the post-70 fate of the Flavian dynasty, recounting the movements and activities of the individual dynasts (7.1–120), then describing their reunion at Rome and acts of joint commemoration of the war (7.121–62). The second major section focuses above all on the fates of those few militant rebel Jewish groups and individuals who persisted in arms after the fall of Jerusalem, first in Judaea itself

(7.163–406), and then in the Diaspora (7.407–53). The two outstanding narratives of the book are the account of the Flavian triumph, in the Flavian section of the work, and, in the rebels section, the story of the collective suicide of the sicarian defenders of Masada.

The travels of the Flavians, recounted early in the book, emphasize the salvific nature of the new dynasty, bringing the blessings of peace and order to the whole Roman world. Rome and Italy show no signs of the recent civil war, described by Josephus himself back in Book 4: instead of division and ruin, we witness the Roman people, of all classes, coming together around the figure of the new *princeps* and affording him a universal welcome (7.21–2, 63–7). Titus tours the cities of the east as far as the Euphrates, bringing largesse and dispensing justice as he goes (7.1–20, 23–42, 96–119). Domitian heads west, supposedly on an expedition to quell rebellion in Gaul (7.75–88). Thus the Flavians, the salvific terminators of στάσις in both Judaea and Rome, bring order to a troubled world. Finally, in 71, they reunite in Rome for Josephus' dizzyingly sensory and remarkably vivid, if coldly unemotional, representation of the triumphal procession of Vespasian and Titus.[53] His readers look on as Vespasian and Titus restage the conflict which Josephus has already restaged in the preceding books, in a vivid narrative which emphasizes the procession's artificiality, richness, and spectacle (7.134–5):

Silver and gold and ivory objects of every kind were paraded, and they seemed to the spectators less like a procession of objects than a moving river, so to speak. Tapestries of purple with vivid Babylonian decorations were also on show; translucent precious stones, some set in golden crowns and others in other objects, were carried past in such great abundance that it seemed foolish ever to have believed that any of them were rare.

Some scholars have argued that the number of discrepancies between the Flavian representation of the war (as narrated by Josephus) and Josephus' own earlier narrative is designed to expose the artificiality of Flavian commemoration of the war.[54] Be this as it may, it is hard to deny that the vivid representation of all this splendour serves to depict the Flavians as strongly established masters of the empire, and as generous benefactors to the imperial capital.

---

[53] On the triumph in Josephus, see Beard 2003; Ash 2014; Mason 2016a: 20–30; Davies 2023: 197–202.

[54] Mason 2016a: 27–30; Davies 2023: 197–202.

In the rebel section of the book, Josephus begins by describing the successful Roman capture of four strongholds still in rebel hands outside Jerusalem, by far the most famous of which is Madasa, the remarkable and dramatic Herodian palace on a ship-shaped rock near the Dead Sea, which had earlier been captured by the *sicarii*. He narrates how a Roman army commanded by Flavius Silva invest the rock, building a ring of camps around it, before constructing a vast ramp for their siege engines. On the night after the Roman ram penetrates the walls, the sicarian leader, Eleazar ben Yair, gathers the defenders and urges them to collective suicide, arguing that God has abandoned the Jewish people, as evidenced by the destruction of Jerusalem, and that death would be preferable to slavery. His rhetoric eventually persuades them. When the Roman forces enter the plateau on the following morning, they are astonished to find the defenders dead, with the exception of two women and five children, who hid in a cistern rather than joining the suicide pact and so lived to tell the tale (7.252–406).

The account of the siege of Masada has attracted a good amount of scholarship. The focus of most of that scholarship has been on questions of the accuracy and historicity of Josephus' narrative, principally assessed by comparing his account to the details of the extensive archaeological work on the Masada site.[55] There is no strong consensus overall, but some agreement exists that he seems to get many of the details of the siege itself basically right, but there is no unambiguous evidence for the mass suicide (although this does not necessarily mean that it did not happen).[56] Some scholars who have taken a more literary approach have explored the possible political resonances of Josephus' account of this episode in Flavian Rome, a context in which suicide as an assertion of freedom had some bite, thanks to the activities of the so-called Stoic Opposition, involving the suicides of prominent figures as a form of protest against Flavian autocracy.[57] Suicide is also a major theme in Flavian literature, and some contemporary parallel texts (especially Silius Italicus' account of the mass suicide of the defenders of Saguntum) resonate powerfully with Josephus' account.[58]

But the greatest disagreements centre on the question of Josephus' tone. The traditional reading is that Josephus holds up the *sicarii* as

---

[55] E.g. Richmond 1962; Yadin 1966; Eshel 2009.
[56] For a good recent overview, see Magness 2019, esp. 5–25, 163–200.
[57] Ladouceur 1987; Mason 2009.
[58] Hulls 2018.

paradigms of courage, having no choice but to admire their courageous last stand despite his general distaste for this faction. However, some scholars have questioned this.[59] Josephus' tone, when recounting the actual suicide, hardly seems admiring (7.389–90):

> Eleazar wanted to say more, but the others interrupted him, all overcome with the irresistible urge to do the deed as quickly as possible. They rushed off as if under demonic possession, each eager to act faster than the next man, believing that not delaying would be a proof of their courage and zeal. Thus they were gripped by a powerfully intense passion to butcher their wives and their children and themselves.

The language of possession and urges and intense passions and butchery scarcely seems to express approval: elsewhere, this is terminology which Josephus deploys when describing the transgressions of the rebels. In his speech, Eleazar himself vituperates the *sicarii* as the first to introduce στάσις and the murder of their countrymen to Roman Judaea: it seems wholly appropriate, then, that they should end their time murdering their fellow Jews. Yet, however we read Josephus' ambivalent tone, one feature of his Masada narrative which must have leaped out at his Jewish readers is the shocking claim of Eleazar that the ruin of Jerusalem demonstrated that God had permanently abandoned the Jewish people. This nihilistic theology effectively amounts to the end of Judaism, and urgently required correction before the close of the book.

Indeed, it gets correction. In the final episode of Book 7, Josephus re-enters his narrative as a character (7.437–53). A refugee *sicarius* called Jonathan makes his way to Cyrene, where he agitates the local Jewish population. Catullus, the Roman governor, apprehends him but then, desiring to increase his reputation by waging his own Jewish war, he colludes with the prisoner to execute local Jews after falsely accusing them of being Jonathan's accomplices, before mendaciously claiming that a number of Alexandrian and Roman Jews were also involved. Josephus himself was among the accused. When Catullus arrives in Rome, Vespasian and Titus see straight through the plot: they dismiss the charges against Josephus and execute Jonathan, scourging him and then burning him alive, but they allow Catullus to get off with a reprimand. However, God intervenes to correct this miscarriage of justice. He strikes Catullus with a terrible

---

[59] Vidal-Naquet 1978; Ladouceur 1987.

terminal illness, in the final stages of which he hallucinates that he is suffering the exact same punishments as the wicked Jonathan. Thus Josephus shows us that, contrary to Eleazar's pessimistic theology of God's final abandonment of the Jewish people, God still cares for righteous Jews, and will still intervene in history to protect them. As in Book 6, Josephus ends by sowing a seed of hope for his Jewish readers: God is still there, still watching and listening, still caring for Israel. Those who state otherwise stand refuted. All this will pass.

What is remarkable about Book 7 is how reassuring it is. General readers are shown first of all that the Flavians have restored peace, order, and good governance to Rome itself and to the wider world; later, they see that the final embers of Jewish rebel ideology have been fully extinguished. Jewish readers, too, will find consolation in that closing anecdote about Catullus and Jonathan – clear witness that God's covenant still holds and that pessimists like Eleazar are misguided. Every kind of reader of the *Jewish War* can find a happy ending in Book 7. And this starkly distinguishes it from Book 6, which, despite its (implicit) seed of hope, ends in ruin, catastrophe, and defeat for the Jewish people.

I mentioned in the introduction to this chapter the contested possibility that Book 7 was a later addition to an earlier version of the work which concluded at the end of Book 6.[60] The implications of that possibility are perhaps more serious than is often realized. The way that a work of historical narrative ends is extremely important, often retrospectively determining the character of the entire work. To borrow Hayden White's categories of types of emplotment of historical narrative, a *Jewish War* which ends at the conclusion of Book 6 would be fundamentally tragic, ending in ruin but incorporating the possibility of growth and progress through suffering for those who survived the cataclysm. A *Jewish War* which ends at the conclusion of Book 7 has been fundamentally transformed into a comic history, a narrative in which order has been restored after its interruption, the wicked have been punished and the innocent vindicated, and all is well with the world.[61]

---

[60] See above, pp. 26–7.
[61] White 1973: 7–11, 163–90, 191–229.

III HISTORY REPEATING: THE *JEWISH ANTIQUITIES*

Introduction

In the prologue to the *Jewish War*, Josephus, justifying his decision to write a contemporary history, takes a moment to scorn those who presume to write histories of the remote past (*BJ* 1.13–14):

> These [Greek historians] might claim superiority in eloquence, but they are deficient in their conception of history. They write about Assyrians and Medes, as if these topics had been recounted with insufficient skill by the authors of former ages. But in reality, they are as far inferior to the early authors in the power of their writing as they are in the soundness of their understanding.

This is, of course, rhetorical positioning, Josephus staking out his territory and defining what kind of history the *Jewish War* is going to be. We should not, then, hold against him the fact that the next historical work which he would produce, the massive *Jewish Antiquities*, would be precisely the kind of history which is decried here, a *longue durée* account of his people's past, extending all the way back to the creation of the universe, much of it based on pre-existing literary narratives written much closer to the events described (and, indeed, prominently featuring Assyrians and Medes).

Josephus was not the only ancient historical author who attempted to write such a sweeping work, and the *Jewish Antiquities*, at twenty books, is not among the longest of such known compositions; nonetheless, it is one of the most ambitious and extensive works of classical historiography to survive entire, offering a magisterial, if somewhat rambling and uneven, sweep through (on Josephus' own reckoning) five thousand years of history (*AJ* 1.13; *C.Ap* 1.1). The tight Thucydidean economy which characterized the *War* is gone. This is a different kind of history, with different models and different ambitions, and different rules apply.

The work can be confidently dated, as Josephus himself concludes it by noting that the present time is 'the thirteenth year of the reign of Domitian Caesar and the fifty-sixth of my life', in other words 93–4 CE (*AJ* 20.267). The reigning emperor at the time, Titus' younger brother Domitian, did not have as strong a connection to Josephus as his two predecessors: he had been in his late teens during the Judaean rebellion and had stayed in Rome. Perhaps as a consequence of this relative distance, the *Antiquities*, unlike the *War*, is not addressed to the Flavian dynasty.[1] Its addressee, rather, is one Epaphroditus (*AJ* 1.8–9), a wealthy patron of learning, probably a freedperson with an interest in Judaism (the same man would also be the dedicatee of the later *Against Apion*; *C.Ap* 1.1).

The broad structure of the work is as clear as its date. The narrative is Temple-centric, with Book 10 culminating in the destruction of the First Temple, and Book 20 ending just prior to the outbreak of the revolt that led to the destruction of the Second, making the *Antiquities* a work of two halves. The hinge which connects the two halves is the figure of the prophet Daniel, who dominates the end of Book 10 (10.186–281), a man who lived through the destruction of the First Temple and explicitly foresaw the destruction of the Second (10.276). This Temple-centric structuring suggests tendencies of historical interpretation which we have already seen in evidence in the *Jewish War*: it implies recurrence in history, and it specifically parallels the destruction of the First Temple by Babylon with the destruction of the Second Temple by Rome.[2]

The first half is predominantly an exercise in reworking the Hebrew Bible, with occasional help from non-biblical sources, but Josephus' book divisions do not usually correspond to the biblical books, giving this history its own, Josephan rather than biblical, architecture. Books 1–4 correspond to the Torah and describe the primordial history of the world and the history of Abraham's descendants down to the death of Moses. Book 5 narrates the Israelites' conquest of the land of Canaan. Books 6–10 focus on the emergence and fate of the monarchy and the kingdoms of Israel and Judah, up to the destruction of the Temple and the Babylonian captivity. Thus, the first half of this block of books describes the establishment of the nation, and the second its fate and eventual dissolution and destruction. Book 11 picks up in the Persian period, describing the reconstruction of the Temple and the restoration of the people, up to the conquest of Alexander. Book 12 discusses the liberation movement under the Maccabees. Books 13–20 follow the fortunes of the people under

---

[1] See above, p. 9, for the possible significance of this.
[2] See above, pp. 45–6.

Hasmonaean, Herodian, and Roman rule up to 66 CE. Thus, the material related in Books 12–20 contains significant overlap with the first two books of the *Jewish War*, which chart the period prior to the Jewish Revolt extending back to the Maccabees, although the *Antiquities* versions of this material tend to be more expansive, reflecting the greater scope of the later work.

One key difference between Josephus' practice in his two major works relates to the citation of sources. In the *War*, he follows Thucydidean precedent in not openly discussing sources. The *Antiquities*, by contrast, is extremely loquacious and transparent about its sources, reflecting the conventions of larger-scale Graeco-Roman histories. We should not assume that Josephus openly acknowledges every source he used; nonetheless, his new-found habit of citation allows us to identify at least some of the material which he knew and used when putting his *magnum opus* together. Unsurprisingly, the major sources on which he relies in the first half of the work are the books of the bible (he seems to have known both Hebrew and Greek versions).[3] Indeed, he repeatedly claims (e.g. *AJ* 1.5; 1.17; 10.281) that the first part of his history is a 'translation' of the Hebrew Bible, neither adding nor taking away from the text, although the work is clearly more creative and interventionist than this formulation might suggest.[4] Biblical material is often restructured (including by inserting elements from the prophetic books into the chronologically appropriate part of the historical material); embarrassing elements are omitted; and material from other sources (Greek historians and the so-called 'barbarian' historians of the Hellenistic period, above all the Babylonian author Berossus and the Egyptian Manetho) is quoted and inserted, either to support the biblical narrative or to be corrected or refuted.[5] Commentary in the authorial voice (not a feature of the biblical historical books) further ensures that what we get communicates a strongly Josephan perspective, distinct from the biblical sources. Parabiblical legendary material is also introduced, whether from oral or literary sources. Some of the sources of the legendary material survive (for instance, the additions to the Greek

---

[3] Nodet 1996; Rajak 2009: 252–3.

[4] On the terminology which Josephus uses for 'translation' (which actually indicates creative reworking), see L. Feldman 1998a: 44–6 and 2000: 3–4.

[5] Extensive discussion of Josephus' rewriting of biblical narrative is provided in L. Feldman 1998a and b. Other helpful studies include Begg 1993; Maier 1994; Mason 1994; Dormeyer 2005; and Westwood 2023.

version of Esther), while others do not (such as the traditions of Moses as a military commander in Ethiopia).[6]

Thus, the biblical half of the *Antiquities* follows identifiable principal sources, the historical books of the bible, but regularly supplements, expands, and checks this material with reference to diverse additional sources. Though Josephus' source material is unusual in the Graeco-Roman historiographical tradition, this procedure – relying principally for factual content on one source per section but reworking and supplementing it extensively – was not, and it seems that the same procedure was followed by a number of Greek and Roman historians who attempted *longue durée* histories, such as Livy.[7]

Some of Josephus' principal sources for the second half have also survived. Book 12 is dominated by sections mainly based on two important Jewish texts of the Hellenistic period, though reworked and supplemented: the *Letter of Aristeas* (*AJ* 12.11–118) and 1 Maccabees (12.237–13.220). Principal sources for the later books do not survive, but Josephus frequently cites Greek authors (especially Strabo, Polybius, and Nicolaus) for his Hellenistic history in Books 13 and 14. The history of Nicolaus of Damascus was very likely his principal source for the reign of Herod in Books 15–17 (Nicolaus lived at Herod's court, and seems to have devoted significant space to that king in his lost universal history).[8] There are signs of engagement with Latin, as well as Greek, historiography: Josephus cites Livy in Book 14 (14.68), and his account of Caligula's assassination in Book 19 (19.1–113) very likely goes back to lost works of Roman historiography.[9] He also quotes Hellenistic and Roman decrees, letters, and documents (some genuine, some of questionable authenticity) with some regularity: he may have used compilations of copies of such material.[10] Finally, his own earlier *Jewish War* can perhaps count as a source for the latter half of the *Antiquities*, given that so much of the same ground is gone over in Books 1 and 2 of that work.[11] It seems likely that, despite the lack of

---

[6] On Josephus' Esther narrative (*AJ* 11.184–296), see Kneebone 2013; on the Moses episode (*AJ* 2.238–53), see Petitfils 2014; Westwood 2022.
[7] Walsh 1961: 138–45; Luce 1977: 139–229.
[8] On Josephus and Nicolaus, see Toher 2003; Czajkowski and Eckhardt 2021.
[9] For Caligula, see Goud 1996; Wiseman 2013: xix–xxvi.
[10] On Josephus and the documents, see Pucci ben Zeev 1998.
[11] On the relationship between the overlapping portions of the *War* and the *Antiquities*, see Cohen 1979: 48–67.

biblical sources for the later books, Josephus follows fundamentally the same procedure here as in Books 1–10, with a single major source for each narrative section which is extensively reworked, transformed, editorialized, and supplemented from elsewhere.

Some interpreters have seen the second half of the *Antiquities* as hack-work. Fluctuations in Josephus' Greek style, together with a proliferation of unfulfilled cross-references, have led some to conclude that *Antiquities* 12–20 is a cobbled-together patchwork of passages taken almost verbatim from now-lost sources and stitched together rather uncritically by Josephus.[12] However, such a reconstruction of the author's practice seems uncharitable. In the large stretch of the *Antiquities* where it is possible for us to compare Josephus with his sources, we do not find uncritical verbatim copying and pasting; rather, we encounter a thoroughgoing and thoughtful process of reinterpreting, rewriting, and reframing, transforming heterogenous sources into a unified work with a singular vision. The intellectual framework of the *Antiquities* remains coherent and singular in the second half, and it seems unfair to imagine that, at the very moment when Josephus' sources become unrecoverable to us, he changed his authorial practice and became an uncritical plagiarist. Thus, the modern consensus is that, though based on multiple earlier texts, the *Antiquities* reworks them significantly and ought to be attributed, emphatically, to Josephus and not to his sources.[13]

Although the *Antiquities* was a very distinctive project, Josephus seems to have been conscious of parallels with several precursor texts and traditions. Most obviously, his repeated presentation of the work as a faithful translation of the Hebrew Bible into Greek makes the first half of the *Antiquities* a parallel endeavour to the Septuagint. Indeed, Josephus acknowledges this parallel early in the preface, when discussing his own quest for evidence that Gentile readers might be interested in this story (1.10–12):

> I discovered that the second Ptolemy, a king who was particularly passionate about education and the collection of books, was exceedingly enthusiastic about translating our law and its associated political constitution into the Greek language. At the same time, [the high priest] Eleazar, who was second in excellence to none of our high priests, did not begrudge that king this favour: he would surely have refused if it were not in keeping with our established traditions to share our good things with others.

---

[12] (Largely) D. Schwartz 2016; Czajkowski and Eckhardt 2021.
[13] Tropper 2016: 63–105; Mason's introduction to L. Feldman 2000.

And so I decided that it was fitting for me to follow the example of Eleazar's generosity, believing that there are still today many people like Ptolemy who are eager for knowledge.

Later, too, when recounting the story of the Septuagint's translation, he conspicuously uses the same language that he applies to his own project, particularly noting that nothing was added to or subtracted from the text (12.11–118, esp. 108).

Greek historiography also presented precedents and parallels for this project. The tradition of writing local histories, focused chronicles of particular peoples or communities, was very well established in the Greek world, and Josephus indeed shows good knowledge of Greek local historiography in the *Against Apion* (*C.Ap* 1.15–18).[14] Specific, and highly relevant, variants of local historiography were the autoethnographic histories of certain 'barbarian' authors written for the Greek-speaking world, a tradition which was initiated in the early Hellenistic period by Berossus and Manetho.[15] Josephus quotes frequently and extensively from these authors and, at least in *Against Apion*, presents himself as someone working in the same tradition as them, although the *Antiquities* was significantly more ambitious in scale than either of their works (both Berossus and Manetho told the histories of their peoples in three books).[16]

A succession of Jewish authors whose works now only survive in fragments (with the exception of the works of Jason of Cyrene, preserved in epitomated form as 2 Maccabees) had written Jewish history and chronography in the style of Greek historiography prior to Josephus: Eupolemus, Artapanus, Demetrius the Chronographer, and others.[17] Josephus does not cite these authors, but he may well have known of them, and perhaps may even have envisioned the *Jewish Antiquities* as the greatest monument and achievement of this genre (it is considerably greater in scope than any known prior work of Hellenistic Jewish historiography). Finally, large-scale totalizing histories of Rome were becoming common in Josephus' time, best represented today by the works of Livy and Dionysius of Halicarnassus, and may have furnished an example to an author attempting a similarly large-scale history of a

---

[14] On the tradition in general, see Clarke 2011.

[15] For these authors, see Sterling 1992: 103–35; Labow 2005: 58–72, 126–32; Haubold et al. 2013. The fragments and *testimonia* of both are conveniently collected in Verbrugghe and Wickersham 1996.

[16] Like Josephus, these authors remain badly understudied by classicists. On Josephus' self-positioning with respect to them, see Davies 2024.

[17] On this tradition, see Sterling 2007.

different people. Dionysius, in particular, has been cited as a significant model for Josephus.[18] His *Roman Antiquities* has a similar title to Josephus' work: both authors identified their works as ἀρχαιολογία (usually rendered as 'Antiquities' in English), histories of origins and early times.[19] Like the *Jewish Antiquities*, Dionysius' work was divided into twenty books. Nevertheless, close and precise parallels between the two texts are hard to find, and Josephus never refers to Dionysius, despite his frequent citation habits in his work, potentially casting doubt on the idea of a close relationship.

Finally, some reflection on the purpose of this huge undertaking may be in order. In the Book 1 preface, Josephus offers us two motives for writing the work (1.5, 14–15):

I decided to attempt the present work because I believe that it will evidently benefit the Greeks to read it, since it will encompass our entire ancient history and describe the arrangement of our political constitution, translated directly from the Hebrew writings.

Overall, anyone who reads this work will learn above all that people who zealously attend to the will of God and do not dare to transgress excellent established laws will meet with unbelievable success in all things, and will be blessed with happiness by the deity. Conversely, for those who deviate from accurately following his laws, the possible becomes impossible, and whatever good thing they envision and try to achieve will result in unmitigated catastrophe.

The first quotation envisages the *Antiquities* as an act of service to a Greek-speaking audience, which could, of course, be complex and broad, including Greeks, Jews, Romans, and many peoples of the eastern Mediterranean. The service comes, it seems, from the work's status as a translation of the 'Hebrew writings': thus, the *Antiquities* aims to make accessible to Greek speakers historical records not in their language. We can relate this to the epistemological landscape of historiography and ethnography in the Roman world, a world in which knowledge about 'barbarian' peoples was always predominantly furnished to the 'educated' public by Greek or Greek-style scholarship. Josephus, then, promises his readers access to an unknown version of Jewish history, and perhaps, by implication, correction of erroneous Greek notions in circulation.[20] Moreover, as we will soon see, he

---

[18] See Cowan 2018, with references to earlier scholarship there.
[19] On the significance of the term, see Rajak 2001: 241–55.
[20] See, for example, Berthelot 2003: 322–55 on how parts of Josephus' work seem directed at challenging the widespread Gentile prejudice of Jewish misanthropy.

takes steps to ensure that his account conforms to Graeco-Roman historiographical conventions, and to make the principal figures of Jewish history seem appealing according to Graeco-Roman standards. This reinforces the impression that one of the motivating objectives of the *Antiquities* is to sell non-Jewish readers on a positive (and unfamiliar) version of Jewish history, rooted in Jewish sacred texts.

The second passage suggests a theological-moral purpose here, too. Those who are obedient to God's will and to tradition prosper; those who are not, fail. Throughout the work, Josephus will depict God rewarding virtue and punishing vice; however, such universalizing tendencies are qualified by his insistence on the importance of Jewish law, and by occasional claims that God has a special care for Israel.[21] A number of Josephus' interventions into the biblical narrative suppress material which may call God's justice into question, implying that he took this moral dimension seriously. Jewish readers may have found additional comfort in Josephus' validation of the importance of Torah, as well as the implications of the recurrent patterns he identifies in history, particularly the Rome–Babylon parallelism (as he also did in the *Jewish War*). In summary, then, the *Jewish Antiquities* sets out to present its readers with a version of Jewish history derived from Jewish, rather than Greek, sources. However, aware that this version of history will seem novel and perhaps unappealing to non-Jewish readers, Josephus shapes the narrative to render it attractive to those familiar with Greek historiography. At the same time, he insists on a just intelligence guiding history, rewarding virtue, and punishing vice, while reassuring Jewish readers that their laws are vitally important and that their people's present troubles are a mere blip in God's eternal plan.

'Remember you were slaves': from creation to destruction

To a putative Graeco-Roman reader of the *Antiquities*, one of Josephus' most puzzling authorial decisions may well have been the starting point. He chooses to begin 'in the beginning', with a paraphrase of the Genesis creation account (1.27–36). Initiating a work of history with cosmogonic material was not at all typical in Graeco-Roman historiography. It may, indeed, be a signal of allegiance to the

---

[21] On Josephus' theology, see MacRae 1965; Attridge 1976; Spilsbury 1998; Price 2011a: 237–42; Klawans 2012: 44–91.

'barbarian' model of autoethnographic history: Berossus began his works with his people's creation myths, as did the later Phoenician historian Philo of Byblos, perhaps making the inclusion of such content a hallmark of 'barbarian' historiography.[22] Josephus then proceeds to recount the rest of the Genesis primordial history, the history of early humanity, and other tales of early mythic history, including the stories of Abraham, Joseph, and Moses, many of which would have been unfamiliar to non-Jewish readers, and which often contain moments of narrative absurdity that may have made them difficult to credit. Nowhere does Josephus explicitly mark a difference between 'myth' and 'history' in his work: the whole account derives, as we are repeatedly reminded, from ancient records which are unimpeachably accurate. Nevertheless, in so confidently presenting material which so many of his intended readers would likely have found outlandish, he creates significant difficulties for his work.

Many of those difficulties would have derived from the established 'knowledge' of putative non-Jewish readers. Greek antiquarian scholarship, a long-standing tradition before Josephus' time, had created reconstructions of early human history, and the prestige that attached to Greek scholarship under Rome ensured that those reconstructions had travelled far and become authoritative.[23] Greek authors demonstrate an awareness that 'barbarians' have their own stories about early history, and some of them (notably Herodotus) demonstrate genuine curiosity about those tales, but these 'barbarian' histories did not enjoy equal prestige or authority in Josephus' intellectual world.[24] The Greek tradition was derived, ultimately, from Greek myth, from the meticulous correlation and comparison of different local traditions, often rationalized, to produce tales of early humanity which were decidedly Hellenocentric, based on Greek stories and Greek heroes. Foreign peoples came to be incorporated into these schemes by having their origins traced to figures from the Greek repertoire: the Persians were seen as descendants of Perseus, and the Medes as originating with Medus, son of Medea.[25] Authoritative historiographical wisdom thus wrote the local traditions of 'barbarians'

---

[22] Berossus: *BNJ* 680 F1a. Philo of Byblos: Euseb. *Praep. evang.* 10.
[23] On Roman receptivity to such Greek scholarship, see Cornell 2010.
[24] Occasionally, Greek and Roman authors explicitly criticize 'barbarians' for their supposedly fanciful tales. See, for example, Plut. *Mor.* 857A–F; Strabo 11.6.2.
[25] Hdt. 7.61.3; Diod. Sic. 4.55.5–56.1. Josephus explicitly rejects such Hellenocentric ethnological etymology at *AJ* 1.120–1.

out of their own histories. Already, the *Jewish Antiquities*, with its strong insistence on the reliability of 'barbarian' stories, is emerging as awkward, prickly, and non-conformist, pushing back against the understanding that prevailed in 'respectable' intellectual culture.

Although Josephus does not explicitly distinguish between early and later periods of history, there are manifold signs in the first books of the *Antiquities* that he did recognize the problem that the 'mythic' primordial stretches represent, and that he took steps to overcome possible resistance on the part of his readers. Several times in Book 1 when recounting the creation and primordial history, Josephus introduces his account with the phrase 'Moses says' or similar (1.26, 33, 34, 37), a qualification which he nowhere else makes when discussing material derived from biblical books, and perhaps a strategy of distancing, partially disclaiming responsibility for improbable content. There is also a persistent interest in corroboration, particularly in citing non-Jewish authors (both Greek and 'barbarian') to support more fanciful narratives: he cites the Third Sibylline Oracle in support of the Tower of Babel (1.118); he calls up Herodotus' testimony on the conquests of Shishak (8.260–2); he refers to Greek accounts of the sea parting for Alexander in support of Exodus (2.347–8). Material evidence is likewise pressed into service, with Josephus drawing attention to objects or epigraphic documents which survive from early history 'to this day'; sometimes such evidence is further verified by autopsy, as when Josephus claims to have seen the pillar of salt which used to be Lot's wife (1.203; see also e.g. 1.70–1; 10.264–5).

Josephus also, periodically, concludes a particularly far-fetched story by stating that he is simply presenting material as he found it, and that he leaves it up to the reader to decide whether or not it is true (e.g. 1.108; 4.158; 10.281). This is an adoption of Herodotean practice, but there is an important difference. In Herodotus, such statements are usually a mark of genuine authorial *aporia*, an indication of the uncertainties of reconstructing remote history and the limits of what is knowable.[26] In Josephus, by contrast, they generally follow passages where the author has explicitly argued for the credibility of his narrative: rather than rendering the account's credibility an open question, they mark moments when the author has tried to stack the deck in favour

---

[26] See also Livy 1 praef.6–7, where the author states that he makes no claims about the accuracy of material about the remote past which cannot properly be verified, and will merely record what he finds in his sources.

of belief. The following quotation, about the age of Noah at his death, illustrates this procedure well (1.104–8):

> After the flood, Noah lived for 350 years, enjoying a blessed life, and died at 950. I hope that nobody, comparing the lifespans of primordial people with those of today and the brief span of years which we live, will conclude that these records are false on the grounds that they could never have reached such advanced ages because nobody today lives so long. We should remember, firstly, that they were particularly dear to the deity, created by God himself. In addition, their diet was healthier, so it was natural that they should live so long...I should add that these claims are corroborated by all historians of antiquity, Greeks or barbarians. Manetho the chronicler of Egypt; Berossus, who compiled Babylonian history; and Mochus, Hestiaeus, and the Egyptian Hieronymus, all of whom wrote histories of the Phoenicians, all agree on this matter. Hesiod, Hecataeus, Hellanicus, Acusilaus, Ephorus, and Nicolaus report that the ancients lived to be one thousand years old. But let everyone come to their own conclusions on this matter.

Thus Josephus preserves the Herodotean form, but the force is entirely different. Rather than a genuine indication of uncertainty or a sign of authorial open-mindedness, his use of this formula, coming as it does after a long litany of one-sided arguments and corroborating testimony, simply serves to make the reader who chooses not to believe look obtuse.

Overcoming readers' potential resistance to outlandish material is not the only preoccupation evident in Josephus' treatment of biblical narrative. Presentation of character, too, is changed. Biblical historiography handled characterization differently from classical historiography; some of the key figures of biblical history could be seen to lack virtues which would have been highly regarded by many Greek and Roman readers. And so Josephus reshapes major characters as he finds them in his sources, in ways which seem tailored to the expectations of contemporary readers educated in Greek historiography. The American scholar Louis Feldman devoted much of his career to meticulous and revealing studies of Josephus' characters in comparison with their biblical versions – essential reading nowadays for anyone engaging with this topic.[27] I do not have space here to do justice to this extensive field of scholarship, but one example – the example, indeed, of probably the most significant figure in Jewish 'history' – can well illustrate Josephus' approach to reimagining these characters for his age.

Right at the outset of the *Antiquities*, Josephus strongly insists upon Moses' status as a philosopher (1.18–21):

---

[27] Most of Feldman's key contributions are collected in L. Feldman 1998a and 1998b.

But, since almost everything derives from wisdom of our lawgiver Moses, it is necessary for me to include a brief preface about him, in case readers should be confused about why much of this work, which supposedly describes our constitution and history, concerns natural philosophy. It should be understood that Moses considered it essential above all for anyone who wishes to lead their own life wisely and also lay down laws for others to study the nature of God. Following this, having subjected God's nature to rational scrutiny, the lawgiver's role must be to imitate as far as possible that most excellent model and strive to live up to it. Without this understanding, the lawgiver will not be able to form a correct conception. Nothing that he might write about virtue would convince his readers, unless they were first taught that God, as the universal father and master who sees all things, bestows happiness on those who follow his laws, but sends bitter misfortunes on those who deviate from virtuous ways.

Several things leap out from this encomiastic portrait: Josephus' tendency to present Torah as a political 'constitution' (found throughout his works); his decision to present Moses as a lawgiver, rather than as the recipient of laws from God; the implicit favourable comparison with lawgivers famous from Greek history and legend; but, above all, the strong insistence on Moses' philosophical insights.[28] This plays into those pre-existing positive Gentile readings of Judaism which stressed its philosophical nature.[29]

Later, in Book 2, during the actual account of Moses' life, Josephus includes some extra-biblical legends which concern Moses' military experience. The Ethiopians were pressing urgently on Pharaoh's borders; the Egyptians consulted oracles, through which God instructed them to use Moses as their general; the Egyptians happily did so, believing that he would be killed in action, such were the odds he was facing. But Moses conducted himself with extraordinary competence and skill, successfully routing the marauding enemy and delivering Egypt from dire peril (2.238–53). Moses is also described as a gifted speaker, another essential quality of leadership in Graeco-Roman eyes, as Josephus repeatedly insists (3.13–14; 4.328), even going so far as to suppress biblical references to Moses' speech impediment to make him seem more assured and impressive as an orator.[30]

These transformations of the biblical sources serve to imbue Moses with qualities which he does not obviously possess in Exodus: philosophical insights, military expertise, and rhetorical flair. Such

---

[28] Josephus' 'constitutional' approach to Torah and presentation of Moses as lawgiver will be discussed more fully in Chapter 5 below. An important recent contribution is Westwood 2023.
[29] See above, pp. 22–3.
[30] For the biblical references to a speech impediment, see Exod 4:10; 6:12; 6:30.

endowments were highly prized by Graeco-Roman readers. In order to persuade those readers that the Jews were a worthy people, and that their 'constitution' was a worthy constitution, Josephus needed to make their ancestor and lawgiver an admirable figure according to contemporary standards. At the same time, Greek-acculturated Judaean readers are reassured that Moses can stand comparison with heroic figures of Greek antiquity, even by Greek standards. These carefully calculated transformations of his source allowed Josephus to do all this, and the final result is a Moses who is significantly different from the version in the biblical original.

It is not only the presentation of characters which Josephus tailors to the tastes and expectations of Greek historiography, but the way that stories are told, too. A look at how he handles the biblical tale of Korah's revolt against Moses illuminates his practice.[31] Chapter 16 of the biblical book of Numbers describes how a prominent Levite, Korah, together with his associates Dathan and Abiram, complained against Moses after he appointed his brother, Aaron, to the high priesthood. The whole community is holy, they argue, so who is Moses to set himself and his family above the rest? Korah's allies also complain that Moses had led the Israelites out into the wilderness and failed to bring them into the promised 'land of milk and honey'. In response, Moses suggests that Korah and his partisans, alongside Aaron, should bring censors before the Lord, who will indicate which of them is holy. When they do this, the Lord appears to the Israelites and, at Moses' urging, God makes the ground open up and swallow Korah and his supporters before the whole assembly (Num 16:31–4). In a slightly awkward narrative inconsistency immediately after this, we are subsequently informed that fire fell down upon the rebels (Num 16:35), giving them two different modes of death. The whole episode reinforces Moses' authority and closeness to God, and the correctness of his appointment of Aaron and his descendants to the priesthood.

This story is expansively retold, with substantial elaborations, in *Antiquities* 4, and the nature of those elaborations illustrates Josephus' approach to biblical materials throughout the work (4.11–58). Terminology with Thucydidean resonances, and echoing the terminology of the *Jewish War*, proliferates: στάσις ('unparalleled among Greeks and barbarians') occurs frequently in the account, as

---

[31] More expansively on this episode, see L. Feldman 1998b: 91–110.

well as the language of tyranny, disturbance, and disorder.[32] The question of motivation is interesting. In Numbers, there are essentially two motives for Korah's sedition: that Moses is unjustly seeking to set himself up over a people who are all holy and beloved of God (Korah's associates even claim that the endgame is to 'enslave' the Israelites), and the complaints of Korah's followers against Moses' apparently ineffective leadership of the people in the wilderness (Num 16:3, 14–16). In the *Antiquities*, the rebels' motivation is predominantly explored through rhetoric, both in a long oration, partly in direct speech and partly in *oratio obliqua*, delivered by Korah himself, and also in a fiery collective oration attributed to the people who have been incited by Korah (*AJ* 4.15–19, 22–3). Korah claims that Moses is seeking glory for himself in the feigned name of God; that his bestowing of the priesthood on Aaron by diktat rather than through democratic consultation, like a tyrant, was in defiance of Moses' own laws; that the people must punish Moses before his power grows out of hand; and that more suitable candidates for the high priesthood (tellingly including Korah himself) exist among them. After allowing Korah to outline these grievances in an oration which draws liberally on the repertoire of Greek rhetoric, Josephus makes the following observation in the authorial voice: 'In saying these things, Korah wanted to create the impression that he was solicitous for the welfare of the people, but really his plan was to have the high priestly office transferred to himself by the popular assembly' (4.20).

This interjection reflects two important elements of Josephus' practice when elaborating biblical narrative: the introduction of direct authorial comment, and a psychologizing instinct to explore his characters' inner drives and emotions. It also, of course, reinforces the already-established picture of Korah as a Thucydidean demagogue, or indeed a character analogous to the 'tyrants' of the *Jewish War*. This characterization is underlined by the introduction of Korah, in which it is emphasized that he was a gifted speaker, especially so when addressing the δῆμος ('popular assembly') (4.14). Thus, he is a rabble-rouser, posturing, Cleon-like, as a 'watchdog of the people', while secretly driven by entirely selfish motivations. In addition to Greek parallels, the close of the sentence, about Korah aiming to have 'the high priestly office transferred to himself by the popular assembly',

---

[32] στάσις: *AJ* 4.12, 13 (twice), 30, 32, 59; tyranny: *AJ* 4.16, 22; disturbance and disorder (θόρυβος and ταραχή): *AJ* 4.22, 32, 35, 36, 37, 63. See D. Schwartz 2016: 45; Edwards 2023.

may have reminded some readers of sinister parallels from the history of the late Roman Republic, such as Marius usurping Metellus' command against Jugurtha through a vote of the popular assembly.[33] There is nothing in Josephus' biblical source to parallel this complex, layered, and allusive portrait of rebel motivations.

Nor is there any real biblical precedent for the elaborate rhetoric in Korah's speech. Indeed, one of the most striking differences between Numbers and the *Antiquities* is just how 'rhetorical' the latter is. Josephus enlivens the episode with four orations: one by Korah (4.22–3), one by his followers (4.14–16), and two by Moses (4.25–35, 40–50), more than satisfying Graeco-Roman historiography's generic expectation of rhetorical set-pieces. Josephus also, characteristically, streamlines narrative difficulties in his original, specifically the aforementioned inconsistency on how the rebels died. In his version, the ground opens up and swallows those associated with Dathan and Abiram, while fire consumes Korah and his followers (4.51–2, 54–6). Thus, Josephus preserves both biblical narratives of the deaths of the rebels, while drawing a distinction which eradicates the inconsistency.

We are left with a narrative which is clearly and recognizably based on that in Numbers, but which has been thoroughly transformed for a new audience into a tale which, despite its bizarre *denouement*, conforms broadly to the way in which revolts and rebellions were often handled in Greek historiography, including in Josephus' own earlier work, where a demagogue and would-be tyrant incites the wider populace, for predominantly selfish motivations, to reject the established leadership. These transformations of the biblical source – the addition of authorial comment and *sententiae*, the smoothing of narrative inconsistency, the insertion or radical expansion of speeches, and the heightened attention to psychology and motivation – are typical, and illustrative of the ways in which Josephus makes this sort of material more palatable to Greek historiographical norms throughout the biblical portion of the *Antiquities*.

It remains to reflect on how to interpret these transformations. Traditionally (as in the works of Feldman), such modifications of biblical sources would be read as signs of Josephus aiming to reach out to Gentile readers by reshaping biblical material to their tastes. However, this ought to be problematized. As was shown in Chapter

---

[33] Sall. *Iug.* 64–5; 84–6.

1, by the time of Josephus, Jews in the Mediterranean had been living in a world of Greek cultural hegemony for centuries.[34] The types of narrative transformations we have encountered in this chapter may very well have been appreciated and enjoyed by Greek-educated and Greek-acculturated Jewish readers who knew the 'classics' as well as Josephus, just as much as by any envisioned Gentile audience. It would perhaps, then, be mistaken to interpret Josephus' Greek authorial touches solely through the lens of 'outreach': instead of a manipulative attempt to make the bible palatable to non-Jews, what we may well have in the *Antiquities* is an authentic Hellenistic Jewish reading of ancient texts which aimed to make them speak to both Jews and Gentiles in a changed world.

Chant down Babylon: from restoration to destruction (again)

At *Antiquities* 11.296, Josephus rounds off his retelling of the Esther story and, with that, reaches the end of the portion of the *Antiquities* which depends on biblical sources. Moving forward, he faced a potential difficulty. In his earlier *Jewish War*, he had begun his account of the build-up to 66 CE at the Maccabean Revolt. From that point on (beginning at *AJ* 12.237), Josephus is essentially covering the same material in the *Antiquities* as he had in Books 1 and 2 of the *Jewish War*. The title of this chapter, 'History Repeating', alludes primarily to the Temple-centric structure of this work, to the vision of the destruction of the Second Temple as a repeat of the destruction of the First. But for the latter half of the *Antiquities*, the title could have a secondary application too: the later books require Josephus to repeat the history which he has already written, albeit on a much-expanded scale. So how did he respond to this challenge, the challenge of repeating himself in a way which made his new work significantly distinct from his first?

A case study can illuminate this question. The second half of Book 1 of the *Jewish War* comprises an account of Herod's reign, providing readers with what looks, in essence, like a Greek biography of the king (*BJ* 1.286–673). Josephus is even more expansive when relating Herod's reign in the *Antiquities*: much of the second half of Book 14 is devoted to Herod's youth and rise to power, and Books 15–17 are

---

[34] See above, pp. 15–18.

almost entirely devoted to his reign. The inclusion of material not covered in the *War* accounts for much of the expanded scope: most of the additional material concerns either Herod's relations with prominent Romans (above all Marcus Agrippa) or further details of the conspiracies and atrocities which characterized his reign.[35] More expansive rhetorical set-pieces also account for some of the bloat.[36] But what is most interesting about comparing the two versions is that the Herod of the *Antiquities* creates a significantly different impression on the reader from the Herod of the *War*. Above all, this is to do with differences in how Josephus structures his two accounts.[37]

The *War* biography of Herod is, explicitly, arranged thematically. Josephus begins with a section chronicling Herod's successes in war (*BJ* 1.286–400), followed by an overview of the king's expansive construction programme, itself thematically arranged according to whom each project honoured (1.401–30). Both of these sections are broadly positive in outlook. However, after this he marks a turning point: 'But Fortune took fearsome revenge for his political successes through his private affairs, and his ill fortunes arose from the woman to whom he was most devoted' (1.431). The remainder of the account focuses on the king's dismal private life. At the very end of the Herod account, Josephus provides an obituary notice which similarly stresses and exposes this thematic arrangement (1.665):

In many respects he was as fortunate as any man ever – he became king despite his common birth, he held power for very many years, and he left his kingdom to his children. However, in his private life he met with the most extreme misfortunes.

Thus Josephus is clear enough with his readers about how he has conceptualized Herod and arranged his narrative: the king was a great success publicly, but a disaster in terms of dynastic politics, and these aspects of the king's reign will be dealt with sequentially, rather than in chronological order. However, despite Josephus' openness about this thematic structuring, it is still difficult for the reader of the *War* to escape the impression that what we are reading is, in fact, a

---

[35] E.g. the conspiracy of Costabar (*AJ* 15.253–66); Herod and Marcus Agrippa (*AJ* 16.12–65); Herod's robbery of David's tomb (*AJ* 16.179–87).

[36] E.g. the expansion of Herod's post-Actium speech to Augustus at Rhodes from three chapters (*BJ* 1.388–90) to six (*AJ* 15.188–93), and the vast rhetorical expansion of the trial of Alexander in Rome from three chapters (*BJ* 1.452–4) to thirty-six (*AJ* 16.91–126).

[37] For a more expansive comparison of the two accounts than can be essayed here, see Landau 2008. See also Van Henten 2011; Bond 2012; Van Henten 2015; Czajkowski 2016.

decline narrative, and this impression derives directly from Josephus' ordering of material, with a litany of glorious successes followed by a long list of acts of tyranny and brutality. The language of tragedy proliferates in the account, figuring Herod as a tragic tyrant, a type which practically requires a decline into tyranny.[38] Josephus' own language can at times reinforce this impression, working in tension with his open exposure of thematic arrangement: note how, in the first quotation above, his domestic troubles are presented as 'revenge' for his public successes, a formulation which surely requires a temporal sequence of success followed by misfortune. In sum, Josephus' structuring of the Herod account inescapably creates the misleading impression of a king who started strong but declined into unrestrained paranoia and tyranny.

This impression is not in evidence in the *Antiquities*, because here Josephus arranges his material chronologically. Thus, by reading the *Antiquities*, we learn that some of Herod's greatest triumphs as cited in the *War* took place late in his reign, and similarly some of his most shocking atrocities happened early.[39] The *War* Herod can neatly be understood as an established stock character, the tragic tyrant, and his life is made to seem as if it fits a familiar sequence of glory and decline. The *Antiquities* Herod cannot be so pigeonholed: here, Josephus gives us a more complex and (to this reader) compelling character, someone who, at all stages, was capable of both visionary statecraft and appalling brutality. In these ways – by incorporating additional material, digressing, expanding the rhetoric, and radically restructuring his earlier work – Josephus provides us with a distinct account from the one he had produced previously, despite a significant repetition of subject matter.

As the *Antiquities* meanders towards its near-contemporary conclusion, one of its most notable features is a tendency, in the last books, towards history which extends far beyond Judaea, and which does not always have a strong connection to the work's theme of the history of the Jewish people. The most well-known instance of this comes in Book 19, where Josephus provides a detailed, vivid, and apparently quite well-informed account of the assassination of the Roman emperor Caligula (19.1–113). This is one of the few parts of

---

[38] Van Henten 2011.

[39] For instance, the murder of the high priest Aristobulus comes early in the *Antiquities* account of Herod's reign (*AJ* 15.50–6), but late in the version that appears in the *War* (*BJ* 1.437); similarly with the execution of his wife Mariamne (*AJ* 15.202–31; *BJ* 1.438–44).

the *Jewish Antiquities* which has attracted serious attention from classicists and Roman historians, in part because an unfortunate gap in our sole manuscript of Tacitus' *Annals* means that we are entirely dependent on Josephus for a detailed account of this significant event.[40] But the Caligula episode is just one of several sections in the last few books of the *Antiquities* where Josephus extends the reach of his history far beyond its core subject: the Caligula assassination is followed by an equally detailed account of the accession of Claudius (19.114–273), and elsewhere in the later books we find lengthy narratives of affairs within the Parthian Empire, specifically the careers of the Jewish 'bandit-leaders' Anilaeus and Asinaeus (18.310–79), and the tale of the 'conversion' to Judaism of members of the royal family of the kingdom of Adiabene (20.17–96).

The theme which connects all of these episodes, both to each other and to the broader outlook of the *Antiquities*, is divine providence.[41] Josephus makes it abundantly clear that, beyond all of the plotting and conspiracies which he charts among the Roman elite, it is his God who is behind the assassination of the emperor (and, indeed, the frustration of Caligula's plan to introduce a statue of himself into Jerusalem, the narrative in Book 18 which provides Josephus with his explicit motivation for including an assassination account in the following book).[42] Similarly, Claudius' accession is divinely orchestrated (19.65–69); providence is also behind the accession of Caligula (18.211–14); in the Adiabenian episodes, God protects the Jewish protagonists from an array of threats and plots (e.g. 20.75–91); and in the case of the bandits, they flourish as long as they follow God's laws, but suffer catastrophe as soon as they depart from them (20.332–40, esp. 340, where the brothers' success is attributed to their adherence to the laws). The universal power and providential direction of the Jewish God, fully on display in these episodes, connects Josephus' account of the history of recent decades with the broad sweep of biblical history which has gone before it, in a unified vision of world history as intelligently guided by a particular deity, the God of Abraham, Moses, and Josephus.

To some readers, this centring of the Jewish God may have seemed inappropriate, especially in the light of recent history. Had not the revolt of recent memory demonstrated clearly the failure of this deity to protect

---

[40] E.g. Birley 2000; Pagán 2005: 93–108; Wiseman 2013.
[41] On Josephus' providential theology, see above all Attridge 1976.
[42] See Davies 2020 for a full discussion of indications of divine orchestration in these accounts.

his own people? What impertinence, then, to ascribe to him control over the highest affairs of Rome! But the groundwork for this conception has been laid throughout the *Antiquities*. In particular, in Books 10 and 11, towards the end of the biblical narrative, Josephus relates Judaea's history as a repeatedly colonized region in terms which would have been very familiar to any reader conversant with Greek historiography. Greek historians since Herodotus had conceptualized the history of Asia as a series of imperial hegemonies and a narrative of *translatio imperii* ('succession of empire'), most commonly passing from Assyrians to Medes to Persians to Macedon to Rome.[43] Josephus configures his account of Judaean history in these familiar terms, taking care explicitly to mark the transitions at the beginning of each new stage in the sequence: the transition of Assyria to Media at *AJ* 10.30; Babylon to Persia at 10.248; Persia to Alexander at 12.1. However, he also makes it explicit that each change of hegemony was orchestrated by the Jewish God.[44] Thus, the Greek notion of *translatio imperii* comes to be fused with a biblical understanding of history: it becomes the vehicle through which God's plan unfolds, as the deity raises up and casts down successive Gentile superpowers in order to punish or redeem his people. And Rome, crucially, is a part of this same sequence.

This is where differences most clearly emerge between Josephus and those possible models of his, Livy and Dionysius, who related the history of the Roman people from their origins to their present imperial domination. Historians of Rome wrote history as focalized through the perspectives of the imperial masters: it becomes a story of the march toward universal domination, which positions Roman rule as the *telos* of human experience. Josephus, conversely, offers world history from the perspective not of the winners but of the losers, the colonized, and that perspective puts a wholly different spin on things. No longer the 'end of history', Rome is just another transient superpower, a temporary state rather than *imperium sine fine* ('empire without end'). Rome has been raised up by the God of the Jews. One day, like its Babylonian analogue and the other great empires in this long tale, it will be cast down in its turn, all in furtherance of an eternal divine plan which revolves entirely around the relationship between God and his people. In this way, too, history repeats.

---

[43] On this scheme, see Drews 1973; Momigliano 1982: 544–6; Lenfant 2007.
[44] Nahum and Jonah predicted the fall of Assyria (*AJ* 9.239–42, 214); Daniel foresaw the fall of Babylon (*AJ* 10.239–44); the rises of both Cyrus and Alexander were foretold in the Jewish sacred books (*AJ* 11.56, 337).

IV HISTORY IN MICROCOSM: THE *LIFE OF JOSEPHUS*

Introduction

In many ways, the *Life of Josephus* is not an edifying or enjoyable read. It has been accused by some of extreme sloppiness, both of literary composition and of factual accuracy and consistency, and at times even of outright mendacity.[1] It raises questions of taste, too. In the modern world, extremes of self-praise are often seen as crass, at least by those of us who are not real estate moguls who become presidents. While it is true that standards differed in Graeco-Roman antiquity, a cultural context in which trumpeting one's own virtues was not taboo, the *Life* seems to go beyond contemporary standards, containing tendencies of autopanegyric which would make even Cicero blush.[2] These grounds for distaste, together with the *Life*'s brevity and conventional status as a decidedly minor work, have meant that it has received rather less scholarly attention than the other works of Josephus. Nonetheless, much of the scholarship which it has inspired has been interesting. That research has certainly made it clear that this text, for all its faults and lapses, speaks to far more than just the inflated self-image of one rather conceited man.

Uniquely among Josephus' works, the *Life* is entirely missing a preface. However, the final sections of the last book of the *Jewish Antiquities* contain a sentence which could effectively function as a prologue to the work (*AJ* 20.266–7):

> Perhaps it will not strike my readers as invidious or inappropriate to give an account of my family history and the events of my life while people still live who can either dispute or support my claims. When I have done this I shall bring my *Antiquities* to its conclusion, comprising as it does twenty books and sixty thousand lines.

The very last sentence of the *Life* (*V* 430) refers back to the dedicatee of the *Antiquities*, Epaphroditus, and claims that Josephus is, at that point,

---

[1] For accusations of sloppiness, see, for example, Mason 2001: xiii, xxix, xlvii–xlviii; Rappaport 2007. For the question of mendacity, see Rappaport 1994.

[2] On Josephus' engagement with Greek and Roman notions of decorum in self-praise, see Glas 2024: 142–83.

reaching the end of his account of 'our antiquities' (ἀρχαιολογία). These factors suggest that the *Life* was originally a part of the *Antiquities*, a sort of appendix in which Josephus, having surveyed the whole history of his people, adds an account of his own life and achievements. Thus, in terms of date, it seems that we can confidently assign the *Life* to the same year as the *Antiquities*, in other words the thirteenth year of the reign of Domitian, or 93–4 CE.[3]

The probable status of the *Life* as a constituent part of the *Antiquities* should influence the way that we read it. The academic convention of treating the *Antiquities* and the *Life* as separate works (to which this book contributes by giving them separate chapters) does violence to the integrity of what was originally a unitary work. Although I follow convention here in separating the *Life* from the *magnum opus*, I will endeavour, in what follows, to be attentive to the connections and shared preoccupations which unify the two texts.

While the text itself emphasizes that it is an account of the whole of Josephus' life, in fact it very heavily focuses on one short period, the six months between Josephus assuming his command in Galilee during the early stages of the Jewish Revolt and the arrival of Vespasian in the area in 67 CE. Such distorted proportions may surprise modern readers, who might expect autobiographies to offer more even coverage, but it was not uncommon for ancient biographies to concentrate on the period of the subject's public life, which was unusually short in Josephus' case.

The work begins by establishing the dignity and prestige of Josephus' lineage, and proceeds to describe his youth and (particularly) his education (*V* 1–12). At chapter 13, he enters public life. There, we find the account of the embassy to Rome (13–16) which was discussed in Chapter 1.[4] Following his return to his homeland, the real focus of the work emerges, the Galilean command. After a brief account of the early phase of the Revolt and Josephus' activities in Jerusalem at that time (17–27), he takes up the mission entrusted to him by the Jerusalem κοινόν ('council'), the elite-led self-appointed 'rebel government' of 66–7, and heads to Galilee. The stated mission with

---

[3] This conclusion is complicated by the fact that Photius, at *Bibl.* 33, claims that the rival history of the Jewish Revolt written by Justus of Tiberius, which Josephus mentions in the *Life*, was written in 100 CE. In the past, this has generated ingenious hypotheses of multiple editions (e.g. Laqueur 1920: 1–127). However, the modern consensus is that Photius simply got the date wrong: see Barish 1978; Cohen 1979: 170–80; Mason 2001: xiv–xxi. For dissent from the consensus, see Kokkinos 1998: 396–400; Kokkinos 2003.

[4] *See* above, p. 5.

which he is entrusted is initially to attempt to win the obedience of the more rebelliously inclined elements in the region: Josephus claims that the elite rebel leaders were playing a double game, and that they were secretly hoping for peace with Rome, but in order to maintain their authority they had to pretend to favour revolt, all the while attempting to rein in the more extreme tendencies of the rebels (28–9). At this moment the narrative pauses, and Josephus briefly drops out of autobiographical mode to sketch the complex political situation in Galilee which he encountered on his arrival, with multiple opposing factions in each city and outbreaks of violence between Jews and non-Jews in various locales (30–61).

This contextual digression ends at chapter 62, and the account of Josephus' conduct of his mission begins there (62–188). The early sections of the account focus on his struggles with various oppositional factions who did not respect or recognize his authority. By a variety of ruses, and by winning the affection of the common Galileans, he is able to outfox his numerous opponents, avoid plots and dangers which threaten his life, and come out on top. His opponents prominently include John of Gischala, one of the principal rebel 'tyrants' of the *Jewish War*, whose rabble-rousing career began in Galilee during Josephus' command.

Close to the mid-point of the narrative, a major new threat to Josephus' authority emerges: the villainous John, exploiting his contacts in Jerusalem and the susceptibility of the Jerusalem leaders to bribery, manages to convince the κοινόν that Josephus should be stripped of his powers. Much of the following section concerns the various ruses by which Josephus is able to avoid the snares of the envoys sent from Jerusalem to accomplish this, and to retain power, ultimately having his commission reaffirmed (189–406). Towards the end of this section, there occurs a lengthy digression on Justus of Tiberias' lost history of the Revolt, which tries to refute that account and to undermine Justus in a number of ways (336–68). Then, at 407, Vespasian and his Roman army arrive in the region, and Josephus declares that he need not narrate any more about his Galilean career, since it has been satisfactorily covered in the earlier *Jewish War*. The book concludes with a brief section which discusses his fate as a Roman prisoner, his post-Revolt life in Rome, the honours shown to him by the Flavian emperors, and his private and familial affairs (407–30).

Modern readers have no hesitation in assigning a genre to this work, the genre of autobiography. However, it is not clear that 'autobiography' was conceptualized as a distinct genre in antiquity. The *Life* of *Josephus* is, as its very title suggests, a βίος, a Graeco-Roman-style biography. Like all βίοι, we should expect its focus to be on the ἦθος, the character, of the subject, and on illustrating his virtues through action – and indeed those expectations are largely met.[5] The work includes many of the standard features of a Graeco-Roman life (a genre which was itself strongly shaped by rhetorical conventions for encomium and invective): sections on ancestry and education; a particular focus on public life, while also including private and domestic details; and the prominence of named and identified virtues in the discussion of the subject's conduct.[6] Josephus' procedure is closer to a Plutarchian than a Suetonian biography, in that his public career (chiefly the command in Galilee) is treated chronologically rather than under thematic headings.[7]

Comparison with other examples of autobiographical βίοι is impossible because of the lack of surviving *comparanda*. Although a number of texts from the Greek world, such as Xenophon's *Anabasis* and Isocrates' *Antidosis*, have marked autobiographical dimensions, it may have been the case that full-blown politically focused autobiographical βίοι really began in Rome in the Late Republic and Early Principate. Sulla's twenty-two-book autobiography was fundamentally influential, and later figures like Augustus, Suetonius Paullinus, and Agrippina the Younger also produced memoirs.[8] So, although we cannot compare the *Life* with any surviving prior example of Roman 'autobiography', we can identify a tradition to which it seems to belong. In terms of comparable texts which do survive, attention is sometimes drawn to Tacitus' *Agricola*, composed a few years after the *Life*.[9] The *Agricola* shares some general features with the *Life*, including its disproportionate focus on a short period of its subject's life, and even some striking close parallels. For instance, when Tacitus, at the moment when Agricola arrives in Britain to take up the governorship (which is the main focus of the work), breaks off to provide a geographical, ethnographic, and historical digression on the Britons, we recall that this is what Josephus does for Galilee on his arrival in the

---

[5] For Graeco-Roman biography in general, see above all Hägg 2012.
[6] On the importance of conventions of Graeco-Roman biography and encomium to the *Life*, see Barish 1978; Cohen 1979: 101–3; Mason 1998a; Gnuse 2002; P. Stern 2010: 77–84; P. Stern 2011: 394–6.
[7] For a different view of the *Life*'s relationship to ancient autobiography, see Grojnowski 2023.
[8] Misch 1998: 231–71.
[9] Cohen 1979: 103–4; Mason 2016b: 65–6.

region.[10] There is no reason to suspect a direct literary relationship, but the similarities between these two texts may tell us things about tastes and trends in life-writing in Rome at the turn of the second century.

This little life: the *Life of Josephus*

As we saw at the beginning of this chapter, at the end of the *Antiquities* Josephus suggests that it would be appropriate for him to inform his readers of 'my lineage and the events of my life' (*AJ* 20.266). At the end of the *Life*, he also makes some remarks which may indicate something of the purpose of the work: 'These are the events of my life; let others judge my character however they wish from them' (*V* 430). Thus Josephus himself presents the *Life* as an informative addition to his great work, covering his whole life and family history, and providing his readers with material upon which to base an assessment of the author's character.

These are simple enough statements of purpose. However, as often with Josephus, some scholars have suspected other suppressed agendas at play. In particular, towards the end of his work, Josephus mentions that, in his lost history of the Revolt, Justus of Tiberias had included harsh criticisms of Josephus' conduct in Galilee, and also impugned the reliability of the *Jewish War* (*V* 336–67). Taking their cue from this, some readers have concluded that the entire *Life* is self-apologia masquerading as autobiography and can entirely be explained as a response to Justus' attacks.[11] Such readings (which are not generally popular nowadays) tend to become all-consuming, to see Justus as the interpretative key that explains almost every feature of the *Life*. Any moment when Josephus celebrates any aspect of his own conduct or virtues should be mirror-read as revealing some of Justus' criticisms. When Josephus boasts that he was immune to bribery, this is because Justus must have accused him of accepting bribes; since Josephus claims that King Agrippa approved of the reliability of the *Jewish War*, Justus must have stated that the monarch was unimpressed with that work; when Josephus claims that he did not abuse his power to violate the chastity of any woman, this shows us that Justus had accused him of rampantly sexually assaulting the women of Galilee. An early

---

[10] Tac. *Agr.* 10–17; *V* 30–61.
[11] See, for example, Thackeray 1929: 16–17; Rajak 1973; Rappaport 1994; Vogel 1999: 72.

article by Tessa Rajak (who later changed her mind on this subject) even goes so far as to assume that criticisms of Josephus which are discussed in the text and attributed to specified groups or individuals within the narrative probably also go back to the lost diatribe of our author's Tiberian rival.[12]

Of course, given the loss of Justus' work, we cannot prove that he did not make any of these many accusations. However, this itself points to a problem with this approach to the *Life*'s relationship to Justus: this sort of reading lacks any form of control whatsoever. As Rajak later noticed, Josephus himself explicitly limits his engagement with Justus to a digression towards the end of the work (336–67), and at the beginning of this digression he appears to signal that it is only here that he is turning to address Justus' claims.[13] Thus the only criticisms of Josephus which we can confidently attribute to Justus are those outlined in this digression. The chief claims seem to have been that Josephus was responsible for forcing Justus' hometown to rebel against Rome and the king (340), and that Justus' history was superior in terms of accuracy to that of Josephus (357). Additionally, *Life* 357 seems to indicate that Justus criticized Josephus' conduct at Jotapata and challenged his literary account of that siege (although, curiously, Josephus opts not to discuss Jotapata in the *Life*). Attribution to Justus of any criticism of Josephus beyond these is ultimately speculative, as is the practice of assuming that the 'real' purpose of the *Life* was to answer his criticisms.

In my view, it is not completely unlikely that the publication of literary works which criticized Josephus, including that of Justus, may have shaped some of the contents of the *Life*. An autobiography is a natural place to respond to such critiques, and Josephus must surely have been conscious of them as he wrote. However, such apologetic concerns do not seem to be key to understanding the *Life* as a whole. I agree with Steve Mason that we need no explanation for the text's existence beyond what Josephus offers us, and the fact that, having completed the surely laborious task of writing the *Antiquities*, Josephus may simply have felt that a celebration of his own life and career was merited.[14] Clearly his life was interesting enough to warrant an autobiographical treatment.

---

[12] Rajak 1973: 357. See also Cohen 1979: 121, which assumes that the apologia in chapters 80–4 is a response to Justus' attacks.
[13] Rajak 1987; Rajak 2002: 152–3. See also Mason 1998a; P. Stern 2011: 387–8.
[14] Mason 1998a; Mason 2016b: 63–4, 72.

But even with all this being said, it still seems that Justus' criticisms rankled Josephus. Josephus mentions in the *Life* that there had been other critics of both his conduct and his history besides Justus (336), and yet Justus is the only one of these critics who is singled out for a lengthy personalized rebuttal. Some scholars have discerned a possible reason for this particular animosity: like repels like and, if Josephus' portrait of Justus is read carefully, it soon becomes clear that he was remarkably similar to Josephus in numerous respects.[15] Like Josephus, Justus was Jewish. Like Josephus, he boasted a fairly comprehensive Greek education. Like Josephus, he came from a leading family, one of the elite clans of Tiberias. Like Josephus, he was involved in the early stages of the Revolt, including, apparently, opposing Rome (or at least the king). Like Josephus, he subsequently fled to the 'other side' (in Justus' case to King Agrippa) and worked closely with the former enemy.[16] Like Josephus, he wrote a Greek-language history of these events in which he himself had played such a large role. As a Greek-educated Jewish participant in the Revolt who saw the war from both sides, Justus could even invoke many of the very same criteria by which Josephus had established his authority to write the *Jewish War*.

Extensive parallelism is evident in the *Life* itself. There may be some merit in reading Josephus' constructed portrait of Justus as a distorted mirror of the author's constructed self. This is seen in Josephus' invective against Justus in the digression, which seems largely based on mirroring. As we have seen, Justus had accused Josephus of forcing the citizens of Tiberias to revolt against their inclinations; Josephus' response is simply to blame Justus for the revolt of Tiberias (42, 340–4). Similarly, Justus had critiqued the reliability of the *Jewish War*: Josephus responds by presenting Justus' own history as a barrage of ill-informed lies and hearsay (357–60).

But it is in Josephus' depiction of Justus' conduct in Galilee as a participant in the Revolt that this mirroring becomes particularly interesting. On a number of occasions, we see Justus being vituperated for essentially the same conduct for which, elsewhere, Josephus praises himself. Thus, at the beginning of the Galilee account, we are told that Justus, the leader of one of three factions in Tiberias, was dishonest

---

[15] Rajak 1987: 85; Rodgers 2006: 177–8.
[16] This reconstruction of Justus as a 'revolutionary' is based on Josephus' presentation, but we ought to note that it is suspicious: as Rodgers 2006: 178 puts it, 'Josephus' assertion that Justus was a supporter of the rebellion is unsubstantiated by the narrative'.

about his intentions: he publicly pretended to be undecided about how to respond to the rebellion, while privately he was hell-bent on revolt against Rome because he believed that he would be able to obtain power from that course of action (36). Reprehensible behaviour, clearly. However, Josephus has admitted by this point that he was himself in Galilee under false pretences, pretending to be an advocate of revolution while secretly looking to control the populace on behalf of his covertly pro-Roman bosses in Jerusalem (22, 28–9). The mirroring between these two attitudes and courses of action is very noticeable. Throughout, when Josephus lies and deploys stratagems, it is praiseworthy; when Justus does the same, it is a sign of his despicable character.[17] One is reminded here of Quintilian's remarks on how cunning orators can, in panegyric and invective, exploit the close resemblance of some vices to some virtues; in his handling of Justus, his Tiberian *bête noire* and alter ego, the Wario to his Mario, Josephus shows himself to be a master of this technique.[18]

Alongside its handling of and relationship to Justus, perhaps the most frequently discussed aspect of the *Life* in scholarship is its tendency to include apparent factual contradictions with the *Jewish War*. Some scholars have attempted to decide which of the two accounts of Josephus' Galilean command, the *Life* or *Jewish War* 2, is likely to be the most historically reliable (generally preferring the *Life*).[19] Tessa Rajak has sounded a salutary note of caution about this. She notes that the two works are fundamentally different. The *Jewish War* has grander objectives and can only afford to devote a small amount of attention to affairs in Galilee in this period, which it must present as simply one aspect of a larger picture. The *Life*, by contrast, has the space to drill deeper, and can take as its central focus Josephus' own virtues and conduct. Given these differences, we should expect variations in what is reported.[20]

Rajak is quite right to emphasize that many of the supposed 'contradictions' which earlier scholarship had identified disappear

---

[17] On Josephus as a master of stratagems and deception in this work, see P. Stern 2010: 84–5. Particularly nice examples involve his obtaining the surrender of Tiberian rebels by creating a phantom fleet on the Sea of Galilee (163–8), and his entrapment and arrest of Simon, one of the delegates from the Jerusalem κοινόν (324–36). On Justus being criticized for rhetorical manipulation, see *V* 36–42.

[18] Quint. *Inst.* 3.7.24–5.

[19] E.g. Gelzer 1964: 299–325; Rappaport 1994. Cohen 1979: 3–8 presents a synoptic overview of both accounts and a discussion of some of the major discrepancies.

[20] Rajak 2002: 144–74.

when considered from this perspective, emerging more as differences of emphasis than as instances of factual contradiction or misinformation. For instance, perhaps the most notorious of these discrepancies involves the nature of the mission of Josephus itself. In the *War*, we are told that he was sent to Galilee to prepare it for war with Rome (*BJ* 2.562–76). However, as we have seen, in the *Life* he is sent on what is fundamentally a mission of peace rather than war; he was sent there (secretly) to control the wilder elements of the population, to encourage them to obey the 'responsible' Jerusalem authorities, and to prevent further rebellion or στάσις (*V* 28–9). However, Rajak notes that later in the *Life* Josephus claims that, when in post, he received a second commission from the Jerusalem κοινόν to protect Galilee (*V* 62). Thus the two accounts do not really contradict each other: the briefer account in the *War* is merely compressed for narrative convenience, with Josephus stating the terms of his second commission as if they were his original orders, perhaps simply because he does not have space in the *War* to dive too deeply into the local *minutiae* of this period. Similarly, in the *War* he claims that John of Gischala was always a troublemaker (*BJ* 2.585–9), whereas in the *Life* he 'admits' that John started out favouring peace with Rome (*V* 43–5). Again, compression may be suspected here: Josephus 'fast-forwards' John's attitude in the tighter confines of the *War* narrative, skipping his pro-peace phase and moving straight to the position he would adopt at a later point. Rajak is right to note that many (though importantly not all) of the apparent contradictions between the *Life* and the *War* actually disappear when those claims are considered in the context of the scope and purpose of the work concerned.[21] The lesson, perhaps, is that, before we rush to accuse Josephus of shameless mendacity, we should always pause first to ask if other explanations for puzzling features of his works can be suggested.

Perhaps more interesting than the question of when or if Josephus lies in the *Life* is the question of the role that lying, deception, and

---

[21] Some discrepancies which (in my view) cannot be explained in this way include the different identities of the Jerusalem delegates (*V* 197–8; *BJ* 2.628); the fact that Josephus consistently claims to have been in command of significantly larger forces in the *War* than in the *Life*; and the claim in the *War* that John was impoverished and of mean origins versus the claim in the *Life* that he was politically influential in Gischala (*BJ* 2.585, 590; *V* 43–5). Moreover, the *Life* at times appears to contain internal discrepancies, too: Josephus claims at one point, for instant, that Justus was absent from Galilee in Berytus after his flight to Agrippa II (*V* 357), yet elsewhere he depicts him as actively inciting trouble in the region during the time when Josephus was in Jotapata (*V* 350–4).

rhetoric play in the narrative itself. They are absolutely everywhere. Both Josephus and his many enemies and rivals are constantly trying to deceive each other. The *Life* depicts Galilee in this chaotic period in almost Tacitean terms, as a highly rhetoricized culture where nothing is as it seems and nobody will openly say what they mean. Everybody plays this game, but of course the hero, Josephus, is the ultimate player.

The best illustration of this important feature of the *Life* concerns an exchange of letters between Josephus and the delegates of the Jerusalem κοινόν who have come to remove him from his post as a result of John's scheming. When the delegates arrive, they learn that Josephus is wildly popular with the Galileans and so, although they are intent on either arresting or killing him, they cannot be open about this objective (216). They write to Josephus, telling him that they have come not to remove him from office but to honour him and punish John of Gischala for plotting against him; they request that Josephus should come to see them in a small village, and they ask that he only bring a few attendants as the village is too small to accommodate a full escort (216–17). Josephus comments (219):

This is what they wrote to me, expecting one of two responses: either I would come without my guards and thus be in their power, or I would arrive with a large escort, in which case they would denounce me as an enemy of the revolution.

But Josephus is far too crafty to fall for this double-talking ruse. He learns of the delegates' true intentions by getting the soldier who brings the letter drunk and wheedling the truth out of him (220–5). Next, he concocts a manipulation of his own. He writes back in ostensibly friendly terms that he is delighted that the delegation has arrived, but that he simply cannot oblige their request. He is currently with the army, standing guard against the depredations of the Roman tribune Placidus. Thus he indicates that he cannot do as the delegation asks, since that would involve him neglecting his commission from the κοινόν to protect Galilee (a very effective way of pulling rank on the delegates). However, so as not to appear obstructionist, he invites the delegates instead to come to him, at a location which he has dictated, and with his loyal army on hand (226–7). This masterful game-playing by the crafty Josephus leaves the delegates with no option but to write back ordering him to come to them within three days without a military escort (228–9). Unable to keep up with Josephus' adroit manoeuvres, the delegates are forced to make plain the intentions which they would have preferred to conceal; in so doing, they abandon their careful rhetorical façade and forfeit the game. Throughout the *Life*, through both manipulative rhetoric and clever stratagems, we see Josephus wrong-footing and outmanoeuvring his enemies again and again, consistently proving himself a master of deception, rhetoric, and guile.

So what of the connections that link this text to the *Antiquities*, the work to which it was originally attached? Here we should remind ourselves of one of Josephus' stated aims in writing the larger work (*AJ* 1.14–15):

> Overall, anyone who reads this work will learn above all that people who zealously attend to the will of God and do not dare to transgress excellent established laws will meet with unbelievable success in all things, and will be blessed with happiness by the deity. Conversely, for those who deviate from accurately following his laws, the possible becomes impossible, and whatever good thing they envision and try to achieve will result in unmitigated catastrophe.

Once this passage has been recalled, it becomes clear that the life of Josephus, as presented in the *Life of Josephus*, conforms perfectly to this pattern. Josephus is eager to celebrate his own virtues, in terms both of general ethics and of his clear adherence to Torah, throughout the *Life*.[22] Conversely, his rivals and enemies are morally abominable. And the result of all this? Josephus' enemies are repeatedly outwitted and frustrated in their aims, while Josephus triumphs again and again. On a number of occasions (typically in episodes which involve his life being in danger), Josephus emphasizes that he was saved by divine providence or intervention (15–16; 83; 208–9; 425). Thus, his life exemplifies in microcosm the grand theological principle underpinning the *Antiquities* on a much larger scale regarding the connection between virtue, adherence to tradition, and divine favour. He makes himself an *exemplum* of the underlying theological thesis of his *magnum opus*.[23]

The structuring of the work emphasizes this strongly. Steve Mason has identified concentric arrangement of narrative threads throughout

---

[22] On good moral conduct in general, see, for example, *V* 80–3; for concerns for Torah observance, see 113 (opposition to forced conversion of Gentiles), 159 (dismissing his soldiers on the sabbath so as not to risk impairing the observance of the inhabitants of Tarichaeae), and 161 (not wanting his soldiers to bear arms on the sabbath). On the importance of Torah observance in the *Life*, see Stanislawski 2004: 18–31.

[23] Mason 2001: xlvii–l.

the work.[24] For our purposes here, the key point is that, as Mason recognized, all of these concentrically arranged plot threads centre on a fulcrum, a mid-point in the narrative which is thus structurally marked as extremely significant. Josephus tells us that, soon after learning that the Jerusalem delegates were coming to strip him of his powers, he contemplates abandoning his command and leaving Galilee. However, he is dissuaded from this course of action by two factors, the pleas of the Galileans, who love and admire him as their leader, and a remarkable dream-vision which he experiences (*V* 208–9):

That night I had a wondrous dream. I went to bed, upset and disturbed by what I had learned from the letter. I dreamed that there stood before me a presence which said 'Cease, man, from grieving in your heart, and cast off all fear. That which causes you to suffer now will promote you to greatness and success in all things. Fortune will be with you, not only in these present difficulties, but in many more besides. So do not be concerned. Remember that you must even do battle with the Romans.'

Readers familiar with the *Jewish War* will surely be struck by this scene, as almost the inverse of the famous 'visions' which Josephus claims that he later experienced at Jotapata, visions which convinced him to abandon his Galilean command in the most extreme way possible, by going over to Vespasian (*BJ* 3.350–2). In the *Life*, this divinely sent vision confirms our hero in his resolve, and he determines to resist the efforts of the delegation and remain in charge. Thus, right at the heart of the *Life* is a claim that God communicated directly with Josephus, and indeed repeated throughout is the claim that God favoured and protected him. There may have been a place for this type of claim in Roman-style autobiography more broadly: Sulla's memoir famously asserted that its subject was close to, and protected by, the goddess Ma-Bellona and other deities.[25] But it is also appropriate in the broader context of the *Antiquities*, of which the *Life* was a constituent part, illustrating once again that God has a special care for the interests of virtuous and pious Jews.

Indeed, one aspect of the *Antiquities* which was not mentioned in Chapter 3 is the prominence of biographical elements in that work. In common with many Graeco-Roman historians, especially of the period of the Principate, Josephus partly resorts to 'biostructuring' in

---

[24] Mason 2001: xxiii–xxv; Mason 2016b: 68–70. Even if many ancient readers could arguably not have been expected to pick up on all of the specificities of Mason's elaborate structure, the centrality of the dream-vision, which is the key point, is clear.

[25] Plut. *Sull.* 9.4.

his sweeping history of the Jewish people.[26] Many sections of the narrative focus on outstanding individual characters who become paradigms for their age: the patriarchs, Moses, Joshua, Ruth, Samuel, Saul, David, Solomon, the rulers of the divided kingdoms, Daniel, Esther and Mordecai, the Hasmonaeans, and Herod all dominate the narratives of their associated periods of history. Thus, although the *Life* is microcosm and the *Antiquities* is macrocosm, we can see that that macrocosm is largely constructed out of an accumulation of biographical microcosms like the *Life*. Bearing this in mind, one possible way of reading the connection between these texts becomes apparent. Josephus turns himself into the spirit of the age, becoming for his times what Moses, David, and Herod were for theirs: the single paradigmatic example of an entire era of Jewish history.[27]

---

[26] On biostructuring in classical historiography, see Pelling 2006; Pelling 2011: 157–9.
[27] Mason 2001: xlvii–l.

V TALKING BACK: *AGAINST APION*

Introduction

The *Against Apion* is not like the other works of Josephus.[1] Most obviously, it is the only work which is not predominantly narrative. Although many of its themes and preoccupations are historical in nature, it takes the form of a rhetorical treatise, and its central mode is not narrative but argumentation. Indeed, it is argumentative in every sense of the word, by far the most outspoken and intemperate of all the author's extant writings. It was written, as Josephus tells us, in response to hostile commentary about Jews and Judaism which he had encountered in the works of some Gentile (in most cases Greek) writers (*C.Ap* 1.2, *inter alia*). Because of the prestige which Greek scholarship enjoyed in the Roman Empire, hostile presentations of Judaism by Greek authors could cause significant issues in terms of broader attitudes towards Judaism at this time, both in Rome itself and throughout the empire. Thus Josephus aims to set the record straight, to combat misinformation about his people which was circulating in influential Greek works, and to present an insider's view of Judaism to a wider audience, in the hope that such a view would replace the often poorly informed notions which prevailed in contemporary Greek scholarship.

Against Apion is the only work of Josephus which cannot be dated precisely. However, it is clearly later than the other extant works, as it mentions them.[2] The treatise must therefore date to the very end of the reign of Domitian, or else to the reign of Nerva and/or Trajan, either in the very last years of the first century or the early years of the second. In addition to questions of date, questions of genre and literary precedent are tricky. The work is sometimes categorized as religious apologetic.[3] Of all such works which survive from the Roman Empire, the *Against Apion* is the earliest. As we will see in

---

[1] The name *Against Apion* almost certainly does not go back to Josephus, and it is not possible to reconstruct the original title (see Barclay 2006: xviii–xxx; Barclay 2016: 80).
[2] *C.Ap* 1.1 (*Antiquities*); *C.Ap* 1.47–56 (*War*).
[3] On the *Against Apion* as apologetics, see Barclay 2009; Hardwick 1996.

Chapter 6, Josephus was pervasively influential among early Christian writers, and indeed some of the very same arguments which he deploys against the Greeks in *Against Apion* can be found in the works of later Christian apologists.[4] It seems likely that the *Against Apion* in fact played a role in establishing the generic conventions of Christian apologetic literature. Thus, rather than working within an established generic category, Josephus may have been pioneering a new one when writing this text, establishing the conventions and expectations as he went. In terms of the influence of generic forms which certainly did exist prior to the composition of the work, Martin Goodman has persuasively demonstrated that Graeco-Roman forensic rhetoric was a clear reference point for this treatise (and, of course, the language of 'apologetics' was quasi-legal in any case).[5] The work's final major section, the idealized portrait of the Jewish 'constitution' (*C.Ap* 2.151–296), clearly owes something to the established sub-genre of Greek political philosophy, which involved analysing and comparing constitutions and lawgivers.

Partly, perhaps, because of a lack of a clear generic categorization, there has been some scholarly disputation about the work's intended audience, and some of that disputation has reflected wider debates about the intended audience of apologetics as a whole. Were these texts genuinely written (as they usually claim to have been) for an outside audience of non-believers, or rather were they written for an 'insider' audience, to provide readers with arguments to use in defence of their religious position and to reassure them that it was intellectually respectable?[6] I do not think that stressing one or other element is particularly productive. Both Jews and Gentiles could benefit from a text like the *Against Apion*; there is no reason to suppose that Josephus would not have been conscious of this, and would not have had both kinds of reader in mind.

After the dedication to Epaphroditus and introduction (1.1–5), three main sections follow. First, Josephus sets out to establish the great antiquity of the Jewish people (1.6–218). He demonstrates this primarily by appealing to and quoting a wide range of corroborating sources,

---

[4] On Christian readers of Josephus, see below, pp. 101–4. For parallel arguments appearing in Christian *apologia*, compare Tertullian's objections to the indignities of Greek mythology (*Apol.* 14) with those of Josephus at *C.Ap* 2.239–49, or the same apologist's emphasis on the great antiquity of Judaism (*Apol.* 19), compared with the first major section of *Against Apion*.

[5] Goodman 1999: 53–5. See also Kasher 1996; Barclay 2016: 79.

[6] On the work's audience, see Mason 1996; Barclay 2006: xlv–li; Barclay 2016: 81–3.

both Greek and 'barbarian', as well as arguing against the reliability of Greek historians. Following this, we come to the core of the treatise, which takes up the second half of Book 1 and the first half of Book 2 (1.219–2.150). (We should note that gaps in manuscript transmission mean that we are missing the original Greek for part of this section, 2.52–113, and here we are dependent on the Latin translation attributed to Cassiodorus).[7] This is the most riotously entertaining portion of the treatise, where Josephus defends his people's traditions from a horde of Judeophobes, summoning up and quoting a mass of problematic anti-Jewish notions from named authors before refuting them, often in scathing terms, demonstrating a flair for biting and sarcastic humour which is scarcely in evidence in his other works. This long section can itself be subdivided into two parts: the first part, comprising the end of Book 1 (1.219–320), sees Josephus take up arms against several Gentile writers; the second, which covers the beginning of Book 2 (2.1–150), finds him concentrating his vitriol on the eponymous villain of the piece, the first-century Alexandrian poet and Homeric scholar Apion, nicknamed Pleistonikes ('Abundant in Victory'). In the final section (2.151–296), Josephus turns from argumentation and invective to encomium, offering an idealized sketch of the Mosaic law (presented as a constitution), and arguing that it is the most perfect constitution ever devised. In the rest of this chapter, I will consider each of these major sections in turn.

Bursting the bubble: Josephus on the inadequacy of Greek historiography

At the beginning of *Against Apion* Book 1, Josephus explains that one of the factors which motivated him to produce the work was that some authors had doubted that the Jewish people were genuinely ancient (1.2–5). In the Roman world, antiquity mattered, especially in matters religious. Clearly it would do no harm to Josephus' cause to establish, as strongly as possible right at the outset of his treatise, that the Jewish people and their traditions were extremely ancient. He does just that, and the means by which he does it are quite extraordinary.

He sets the tone at the very outset of the argument (1.6):

---

[7] On the manuscript transmission of the work, see Barclay 2006: lxi–lxiv; and Leoni 2016: 315–17.

The first thing that occurs to me is that it is extraordinarily strange that anyone believes that we should only pay attention to Greek authors when it comes to the study of early history, that the truth can only be found in their works, and that neither we Jews nor any other peoples in the world can be trusted on this subject.

Josephus has clearly identified here the core issue which he faces: the widespread tendency to privilege the historical scholarship of one of Rome's subject peoples over all the others. He explains that scepticism about Jewish antiquity predominantly derives from the fact that no early Greek author mentions the Jews, an inference which clearly carries the implication that only Greek authors deserve to be trusted on questions of history (1.2). He then sets out to demolish this implication in several ways: by arguing that non-Greek peoples make better historians than Greeks; by exposing the Hellenocentric absurdity of this argument; by offering several reasons why the early Greeks would not have noticed the Jews; and by adducing both 'barbarian' and Greek testimony which supports his claims about the antiquity of Judaism.[8]

Josephus' claims about Greek versus 'barbarian' history are especially uncompromising. Greek history is, he argues, shallow and unreliable. Among the Greeks, anybody can write history (1.37), frequent environmental disasters have erased much from primordial antiquity (1.9–10), and the invention of writing happened strikingly late, meaning that Greek historians have no reliable sources for early history (1.11–14). Greek historians themselves are characterized as privileging style and novelty over veracity (1.27), and their own habit of refuting each other's works is used to demonstrate the unreliability of the entire tradition (1.16–17):

It is not necessary for me to try to educate readers who are no doubt better informed than myself on how many disagreements exist between Hellanicus and Acesilaus about early history; about how often Acusilaus corrects Hesiod; about how the lying statements of Hellanicus are refuted by Ephorus, those of Ephorus by Timaeus, those of Timaeus by later writers, and those of Herodotus by absolutely everybody.

What these Greek authors lack, Josephus explains, is the single most important quality in a reliable historical tradition, συμφωνία ('agreement').[9] Conversely, what we find in the records of the

---

[8] In the latter section, Josephus occasionally passes off Jewish authors as Gentiles, among other manipulations of their testimonies. See Goodman 1999: 53; Barclay 2016: 77–8.
[9] On the importance of συμφωνία to historiography, see *C.Ap* 1.26, 38, 160. For συμφωνία in Josephus' historiographical theory, see Cohen 1988: 1–5.

non-Greek peoples of the eastern Mediterranean and Mesopotamia are authoritative univocal histories which preserve the plain truth, reported not by any hack who fancies himself a historian, but by the priests, the most learned and virtuous among them, the masters of memory (1.28–9). In this way, Josephus prepares the ground for his use of prominent 'barbarian' priest-historians like Berossus and Manetho to support his claims about Jewish antiquity, at the same time as he seamlessly inserts the Jews into the list of 'barbarian' peoples with authoritative historiographical traditions of the remote past.

In fact, what Josephus is doing here is capitalizing on certain tendencies within Greek historiography which went back at least as far as Herodotus and which presented the 'barbarian' priests of the east as preservers of authoritative local records (in other words, he is exploiting a trope from Greek historiography in order to undermine Greek historiography).[10] We might note the likely influence here of Plato's *Critias*, where 'barbarian' (specifically Egyptian) priests are cited explicitly as experts on the history of the remote past in a discussion which also stresses the poor historical memory of the Greeks.[11] And what is really remarkable about this section is how Josephus does not restrict his *apologia* to the Jews alone: he makes the case for the superiority of a broadly conceived tradition of eastern historiography whose records had come to be overlooked in favour of the shallow and inferior historiographical efforts of the Greeks. It would be a stretch to call this anti-colonial solidarity (Josephus advocates for Egyptians and Phoenicians not for their own sake but in order to bolster his defence of his own people), but nevertheless it is an inclusive and generous gesture, showing that Josephus recognized that the difficulties which he faced as a Jewish intellectual in a world which persistently favoured Greek intellectualism were not restricted to him and his people, but were experienced by representatives of many nations under Roman rule.

What this amounts to is a rejection of the imperial intellectual order as upheld by Roman power. Josephus' boldest moves in this section involve his exposure of the Hellenocentricism of Roman intellectual culture by ironically inflicting forms of it on Greeks and Romans

---

[10] For the trope, see, for example, Hdt. 2.2–3, 44, 99; Diod. Sic. 1.12.9; Plut. *De Is. et Os.* 353B. See also Marincola 1997: 108–11. Similarly, by drawing attention to the Greek historiographical habit of denigration of predecessor works, Josephus uses another feature of Greek historiography to undermine it (while, somewhat ironically, participating in that process of denigration himself).

[11] See esp. Pl. *Criti.* 109D–110B.

themselves. At one point, he applies a mirrored version of Greek cultural arrogance to the Greeks: 'Imagine if I dared to question the age of Greek culture on the basis of the absence of any mention of Greeks in our literature. Surely they would mock and contemn me for this' (1.69). Here, he (correctly) notes that it would be intellectually absurd to attempt to argue that the Greeks did not have an ancient history simply on the basis that no early Jewish text mentions them. Why, then, is it not equally self-evidently absurd to doubt the antiquity of the Jews based on a lack of early Greek testimony? The answer is that the absurdity is obscured by Greek scholarship's link with imperial power. Elsewhere, Josephus implicitly inflicts this same Greek arrogance on Rome itself (1.66):

> The city of Rome is not mentioned by Herodotus nor by Thucydides nor by any one of their contemporaries, although it had established its power and enjoyed tremendous success in conquest long before their time. It was only yesterday, as it were, or the day before that knowledge of Rome reached the Greeks.[12]

Like the Jews, the Romans were ignored by early Greek authors. But would any Greek dare, on the basis of this, to suggest that Rome did not have an ancient past? These authorial manoeuvres are highly effective, clearly exposing the epistemic consequences of the privileging of the 'classical' over the rest.

This first section of *Against Apion* is, therefore, more than just a demonstration of Jewish antiquity (something which hardly needed demonstrating anyway). It also represents one 'barbarian' author protesting the marginalization of the non-Greek world and denouncing the dominant models of historical scholarship.

Beating an Egyptian ass: Josephus versus the Judeophobes

The central section of the *Against Apion* involves the serial refutation of specific points made by several named authors, points which Josephus interprets as anti-Jewish. In the second half of Book 1, he attends in turn to the claims of three authors whom he identifies as Egyptian (although, as we will soon see, his ethnic labelling in this treatise can be a little slippery), Manetho, Chaeremon, and Lysimachus. In all three cases, Josephus' objections relate to these authors' presentations

---

[12] The last clause alludes to Hdt. 2.53.

of Jewish origins and the story of Moses and the exodus. The first half of Book 2 continues this argumentative approach, but focuses entirely on one author, Apion. It initially maintains the focus on the exodus, addressing Apion's account of that event (2.8–32). But the discussion soon progresses to different themes, first rebutting some scurrilous comments which Apion made specifically about the Alexandrian Jews and their social and legal position (2.33–78), and then turning to a miscellany of slanders against the Jerusalem Temple and Jewish ritual and law (2.79–144).

The first target of Josephus' refutations, Manetho, is tricky. This author had already been pressed into service earlier in the treatise, presented effectively as an Egyptian alter ego of Josephus, a learned Egyptian priest who faithfully transmitted accurate Egyptian records through which Josephus was able to verify Jewish claims to antiquity (1.73–105, esp. 73 for his presentation of Manetho). Now, some re-evaluation is required. Josephus argues that, when Manetho is transmitting authentic Egyptian records, his works can be trusted, but on the basis of some rudimentary textual criticism, he comes to the conclusion that, at times, Manetho does not simply translate what he finds in the priestly records, but incorporates additional extraneous material, anti-Jewish slanders of no historical value (1.227–9, 287). This complication of the previously wholly positive portrayal of this author seems to mirror a simultaneous re-evaluation of all things Egyptian: although Josephus earlier praised the Egyptians as accurate historians and masters of remote-past memory, from this point on his comments about Egyptian matters (especially religion) will be unremittingly mocking and hostile (e.g. 1.223–6; 2.28–32; 2.65–7).[13] This is because he presents Egypt as the source of much anti-Jewish sentiment. The Egyptians, he explains, disparage the Jews for two reasons: spite and envy. They hate the Jews because they believe that, in the past, the Jews (identified with the Hyksos) ruled tyrannically over Egypt; simultaneously, they see the whole world despising their culture while admiring Judaism (1.223–6). Thus, the ways in which both Manetho and Egypt more broadly are valued in this treatise

---

[13] It is worth noting that the most frequent elements of Josephus' vituperation of the Egyptians (especially his fixation on the idea that they worshipped animals) seem strongly to mirror attested Roman prejudices about Egypt (on which see Smelik and Hemelrijk 1984; Isaac 2004: 352–70). This may indicate that such vituperation was designed to score points in the eyes of Roman readers.

fluctuate according to Josephus' needs. When he can use them to support his position, he praises them; when he has more to gain from mocking, dismissing, or scoring points off them, he damns them instead.[14]

The strategies of argumentation which Josephus uses in this section of the treatise are varied.[15] Most straightforwardly, he points out elements of the stories these authors tell which can be presented as absurd. For instance, Manetho claimed that the pharaoh Amenophis was instructed by the gods to expel the ancestors of the Jews from Egypt, but he instead forces them to work in a stone quarry and later gives them a city in Egypt in which to live (1.260). Why would he do this? According to Manetho's account, Moses was a leper and led a company of lepers, and yet Josephus points out that Moses' own laws are rather harsh on lepers: this constitutes another absurdity on Manetho's part (1.281–5). Elsewhere, he recounts how Apion's notorious tale of the annual Jewish cannibalistic rite claims that 'the Jews' (presumably denoting all of them) were able to consume the entrails of a single Greek man – patently impossible (2.100).[16] Much of his critique centres on the identification and denunciation of these sorts of narrative absurdities.

Josephus is also eager to point to moments in these authors' works which contain contradictions, either internally or with the other texts under discussion (e.g. 1.293–303). This strategy helps to connect this section of the treatise with the first part, in which, as already discussed, agreement (συμφωνία) emerges as his key criterion of veracity in historiography. Note especially his comments on Chaeremon, while discussing how that author diverges from Manetho: 'those who cobble together lies write things which are not consistent with one another (οὐχ ἑτέροις σύμφωνα), and each invents whatever seems best to him' (1.293). A further element, especially visible in the Apion section, is personal abuse of the authors. Lysimachus is so stupid that, when claiming that the Jews originally named their city Hierosylia in commemoration of their own record of temple robbery (ἱεροσυλία), he does not even pause to reflect that foreign peoples do not use Greek words (1.318–20). Apion, meanwhile, is subjected to a broad range of personal abuse, which will be discussed in a moment. These

---

[14] In a similar vein, Josephus is quite happy to cite Greek historians who support his case, despite his resounding denunciation of Greek historical scholarship in the first section of Book 1.
[15] For more on Josephus' argumentative strategies, see Kasher 1996; Gruen 2016: 245–53.
[16] On the cannibalistic ritual, see above, pp. 24–5.

three strategies – pointing out absurdities, identifying contradictions, and insulting the authors – are the means by which Josephus predominantly conducts his argument against the Judeophobes.

No other author is treated as brutally as Apion 'Pleistonikes'. None of his works survive, but nonetheless we know a fair amount about his life and career. He was an Alexandrian scholar and poet who was active in the first century CE. He produced a great deal of (often wilfully controversial) Homeric scholarship. He lived in Rome for a time, where he met the teenage Pliny the Elder and made a bad impression on the emperor Tiberius. He also won prizes in verse competitions in Greece, Sicily, and Italy.[17] Among his literary compositions, he wrote a history of Egypt, probably the source of his material about the exodus as quoted by Josephus. He is also known to have been involved in the aftermath of the violence which broke out between the Greek and Jewish communities in Alexandria in 38 CE: after the violence ended, Apion was part of an embassy to Caligula on behalf of the Alexandrian Greeks, aiming to convince the emperor that the unrest had been predominantly the fault of the Jews (*AJ* 18.257–60). It may have been in connection with this embassy that he wrote his attacks on the Alexandrian Jews which Josephus addresses in *Against Apion*.[18]

One thing which seems clear from this short biographical sketch is that Apion was Greek. He was an Alexandrian citizen; he was selected by the Alexandrian Greeks to represent them before the emperor; he was Greek enough to compete in, and win, Greek poetic contests in Greece. And yet, when addressing his great adversary in *Against Apion*, Josephus will absolutely not concede to him his Greekness: 'He was born in the Egyptian oasis, the quintessential Egyptian, we might say, but he rejected his true country and people and falsely claimed to be an Alexandrian, an admission of the disgraceful nature of his nation of birth' (2.29).

When engaging with Apion, Josephus frequently draws attention to his supposed 'Egyptianness' and uses it as a basis for mocking and demeaning him. And there is something very striking about all this. What Josephus is doing here is the precise reverse of what Apion

---

[17] On Apion's Homeric scholarship, see Dillery 2003. On his encounter with Pliny, see *HN* 30.18 (and Damon 2011). On his impression on Tiberius, see Plin. *HN* praef.25–6. On verse competitions, see Benaissa 2014.

[18] For more on Apion, see, in addition to the works already cited, Van der Horst 2002: 207–22; Jones 2005; Damon 2008.

himself appears to have done to the Jews in his writings, in which he 'reduced' them to the status of Egyptians. There may have been a political element to this in Apion's original context. Many of the disputes in Alexandria centred on the question of the status of the Alexandrian Jews, with the Greeks attempting to convince Rome that they should enjoy no special privileges over the native Egyptians. If intellectuals like Apion were able to demonstrate that, originally, the Jews *were* Egyptians, that could have been seen to bolster that case.[19] Be that as it may, Apion's persistent desire to depict Jews as Egyptians is reflected back at him here. Considering the frequency with which Egyptians were mocked and demeaned in Roman literature, such a depiction may have been damaging to Apion's credibility in the eyes of Josephus' Roman readers.

In fact, this sort of playful ironic reversal is wholly characteristic of Josephus' procedure when dealing with Apion. For instance, he cites Apion as the source of the claim that Jews worshipped the head of an ass in the Jerusalem Temple, and on two occasions he ironically labels Apion as an ass. One of those occasions is especially rich, combining the ironic labelling as an ass with the strong Egyptianizing tendencies and personal and ethnic abuse which we see throughout: 'These are the factors which Apion should have considered, if only he had not been endowed with the mind of an ass and the impudence of a dog, which among the Egyptians is a well-established object of worship' (2.85).[20]

Similarly, Josephus goes on to record how Apion had attempted to use the Jews' historical lack of success in war as a basis for abuse. He then mocks the Egyptians for their own record of constant imperial domination by foreign powers, ironically turning Apion's own accusation back against 'his people' (as Josephus would have it) (2.125–32). Even the circumstances of Apion's death are not beneath Josephus as a source of irony-fuelled mockery. Josephus tells us that Apion had once claimed that the Hebrew word for the sabbath derived from the Egyptian word *sabbo*, meaning a disease of the genitals, because the Israelites supposedly suffered from this condition after six days in the wilderness (2.20–1). Later, Josephus tells us that Apion mocked the Jews for their custom of circumcision (2.137–42). Thus his humiliating account of his adversary's demise is rich, once

[19] Harker 2009: 212–20.
[20] The other occasion is at *C.Ap* 2.115.

again, in irony and mirroring: 'Circumcision became necessary as a result of an ulcer on his penis; the procedure availed him nothing, the ulcer began to necrotize, and he died in excruciating pain' (2.143). The inventor of slanders about genital diseases dies from a gangrenous genital ulcer, the mocker of circumcision is himself circumcised, and the neatness of all this may even have suggested to some of Josephus' readers that it was divine punishment. Josephus turns Apion's whole life and identity into irony, and then he ironizes him to death.

Although no one should doubt the seriousness of Josephus' commitment to these debates, or the importance of defending his people against these insults and accusations, there is something of the playground about all this: the name-calling, the intemperate language, the careless slurs. However, to invoke the perennial excuse of the playground, we should remember that Josephus did not start it. If, in this long central section, our author seems at times to lack taste and decency, then he is only repaying in kind the insults which had long been heaped on his people by the archetypal antisemites of the Graeco-Roman world.

The best of all laws and the best of all lawgivers

The final section of the treatise involves a significant tonal shift. The focus is no longer on vitriolic refutations of hostile critics or on denigrating other cultures; rather, it is on celebrating Judaism and the Jewish law. This section is not entirely without vitriol, but its prevailing mood is celebratory and encomiastic. It begins with a short preface, explaining that Apollonius Molon, Lysimachus, and others had made two specific problematic accusations: that Moses was a charlatan and that the Jewish 'constitution' teaches vice rather than virtue (2.145–50). Josephus states that the best way to refute these allegations is to provide a summary of the laws and an examination of their teachings, accompanied by comparisons with other celebrated law codes. He begins by summarizing and celebrating Moses' view of God and showing how Moses ensured that his laws would thoroughly inculcate his lofty conception of the deity in all who follow them (2.151–89). Then he provides an abbreviated and thematically arranged summary of the contents of the law (2.190–219), before proceeding to comparisons with celebrated foreign constitutions, both real and imaginary (2.220–86). Finally, he delivers a closing encomium, and restates the work's dedication to Epaphroditus (2.287–96).

Despite the changes in tone and procedure, Josephus does take some steps to connect this material to the rest of the treatise, offering continuity via certain through-lines. He frames his celebration of Judaism within an apologetic setting: he claims that he is providing this material in order to refute Apollonius, Lysimachus, and others (2.145–50); he refers to this objective periodically throughout (e.g. 2.182, 236); and he returns to it at the very end (2.295):

> If it has been shown that no one observes these laws more scrupulously than us, and if we have satisfactorily demonstrated that we were the first to use them, then we may safely leave people like Apion and Molon and anybody else who exults in slander and abuse to their own ignorance.

Thus something of the combative tone of the earlier sections is allowed to persist even in this predominantly laudatory part of the treatise. The scathing denunciation of what Josephus presents as the absurdity and immorality of Greek myth also carries some of the bitter tone of the earlier parts (2.242–3):

> Stories like these are rightly ridiculed by the most intelligent of the Greeks. They deride the idea that some deities are young men without beards, while others are hirsute elders; or that some have jobs, with one god working as a blacksmith, another goddess as a weaver, another as a soldier who fights against mere mortals, while others are musicians and archers. Equally ridiculous is the idea that they engage in disputes, and so heatedly that they not only physically fight each other, but even suffer from and complain about injuries inflicted by mortals.

The figure of Moses is central to all three main sections of the work, and thus he, too, provides continuity with what has gone before. Perhaps most noticeable, however, is the prominence of the virtue of συμφωνία ('concord' or 'agreement'). As we have seen, this has featured prominently in both of the previous sections: first Josephus presented it as the central criterion in determining whether a nation's historical record is trustworthy; then he used the lack of it as a basis for critiquing the claims of the 'Egyptian' authors he refutes. In the final section, it is presented as one of the four key virtues which are taught by the Judaean constitution, in opposition to the contention of Apollonius Molon and others that Judaism teaches vice (2.170–1).[21] This provides strong continuity with the earlier sections, and even

---

[21] On the virtues in the *Against Apion*, see Rajak 1998: 231–4. The identification of four chief virtues was already a commonplace in Greek philosophical writings (see North 1966), but the precise combination of virtues which Josephus claims is taught by the Mosaic Laws (justice,

retrospectively bolsters Josephus' high claims for the reliability of the Judaean historical record. If συμφωνία is the key mark of historical reliability and Jews have been instructed in this very same virtue from birth, then surely they must be master historians.

Josephus' insistence throughout this section on the high degree of harmony and unanimity among Jews is in many ways at odds with his presentation of Judaism in his earlier works. In presenting this overview of the Jewish law, he is summarizing Judaism for outsiders, and he did this in his earlier works too, but in a very different way. In the second book of the *Jewish War*, Josephus claims that there are three legitimate 'schools' (αἱρήσεις) of Judaism. The Essenes (who are given an extensive ethnographic excursus) believe in rewards, punishments, and souls possessing 'new bodies' in the afterlife; in many cases, they live together in common-property communities bound by extraordinary rules (*BJ* 2.119–61). The Pharisees, whose doctrines have much clout with the common people, believe in life after death, hold that both providence and free will play a role in human actions, and are good-natured and strive for the common good (*BJ* 2.162–3, 166). The Sadducees, whose doctrines are especially attractive to the wealthy and powerful, believe that God and providence play no direct role in human affairs and that there is no afterlife, and they are harsh and unfriendly, even to each other (*BJ* 2.164–6). This formulation is clear: it communicates a 'philosophical' vision of Judaism to the Gentile world (the sects are described in terms which echo Pythagoreanism, Stoicism, and Epicureanism), and Josephus was satisfied enough with it to repeat it several times in the later *Jewish Antiquities*, with minor emendations (*AJ* 13.171–3; 15.370–2; 18.11–22).[22] And yet there is not a trace of this scheme in the *Against Apion*, where he once more takes up the task of summarizing Judaism for the outside world. Why?

Josephus most likely abandons his three schools model in this work for the simple reason that it is no longer appropriate to his rhetorical purpose. One feature of the model which is rather attractive to modern

---

temperance, fortitude, and harmony) appears to be original to him. Goodman 1999: 57–8 has suggested that the virtues which Josephus emphasizes as being inculcated by Judaism map very closely onto conservative Roman values, suggesting that Josephus may have had one eye on winning approval from a Roman audience. When we recall how the hostile stereotypes about both Egyptians and Greeks in this treatise also closely echo Roman prejudices, we get the impression that, in the *Against Apion*, Josephus aims to suggest that Romans and Jews are similar, and to oppose both groups to Egyptians and Greeks.

[22] On Josephus' three schools model more broadly, see Haaland 2007; Klawans 2012; Baumgarten 2016.

sensibilities is that it emphasizes Jewish diversity. The three schools believe quite widely divergent things, and yet Josephus is happy to present them all, without qualification, as legitimate expressions of Judaism. However, that same emphasis on diversity would be unhelpful in a work which aims to stress the remarkable harmony that exists within global Judaism, harmony which is emphasized in the strongest possible terms (*C.Ap.* 2.179–80):

> Having one and the same conception of God, and differing in no way from one another in our way of life or our values, has enabled us to attain the most perfect ethical concord (συμφωνία) of all peoples. Only among us will no contradictory opinions about God be voiced; these kinds of disagreement are ubiquitous among others, and are expressed not only among ordinary people whose opinions might change with each passing fancy, but are even forcefully expounded by philosophers.

Thus rhetorical exigency requires Josephus to abandon his earlier formulation of healthy diversity within Judaism and replace it with this (wholly misleading) picture of utter harmony and unanimity. Rhetorical convenience may also explain a further apparent shift from his conception in earlier works. Previously, when expressing Judaean political arrangements in terms comprehensible to Gentile readers, he had identified Moses' constitution as an aristocracy (*AJ* 4.223). Here, this will not do. Josephus wants to establish that the Mosaic constitution is the best constitution ever devised. Other nations could claim to possess aristocratic constitutions and so, in this treatise, Josephus goes one better. He coins a new Greek word, 'theocracy' (θεοκρατία), to describe a nation entirely under the rule of God (*C.Ap* 2.164–7). The neologism, to which Josephus explicitly draws attention, further highlights the exceptional nature of the Mosaic πολιτεία ('constitution'), elevating it emphatically above all possible competitors.

In the final stretches of the *Against Apion*, Josephus is at his best when he is in a celebratory mood, hymning, in rather elegant and elevated language, the nobility of Moses' conception of the deity, admiring the passionate attachment and loyalty of the Jews to their laws, and enumerating the virtues which obedience to those laws will inculcate. It is lofty and dignified stuff, and this is surprising as it comes at the end of what has, for the most part, been an obstreperous, impertinent, and aggressive piece of work. Josephus spends most of this exhilarating treatise fighting dirty in the gutter. At least he is able to finish it looking at the stars.

VI JOSEPHAN AFTERLIVES

Receptions in antiquity

If the literary texts which survive from the Roman era are anything to go by, Josephus seems to have been little known among non-Jewish and non-Christian authors in antiquity. There is no clear indication that his younger contemporary Tacitus knew his works. The latter's account of the Jewish Revolt is somewhat confused. For instance, it mixes up the names of Simon bar Gioras and John of Gischala, an error which is unlikely to have been made by someone who had carefully read the *Jewish War*.[1] Similarly, his account of the exodus draws not from the *Antiquities* or the *Against Apion*, but appears to have been informed by precisely the kind of Judeophobic Greek scholarship which Josephus set out to refute in the latter work.[2] Either Tacitus had not read Josephus' discussions of Moses and the exodus, or he was unpersuaded by them. The same seems true of Josephus' other great prose contemporary, Pliny the Elder. Josephus does not feature in the massive bibliography which comprises the opening of the *Natural History* and, although Pliny mentions two subjects of importance to Josephus, Masada and the Essenes, there is no indication that the *Jewish War* was the source of his information.[3] In terms of later 'pagan' classical authors, the record is similarly exiguous. Both Suetonius and Dio mention Josephus, but not as a source or an author: they refer to him as a noble Jewish prisoner who prophesied Vespasian's accession.[4] The philosopher Porphyry mentions the Essenes and cites Josephus as his source, but other than this the Josephan corpus leaves no trace in the later non-Christian classical tradition.[5]

Josephus' Jewish reception is similarly elusive. We find nothing which need indicate detailed direct engagement when we turn our attention to Late Antique Jewish texts in Hebrew and Aramaic, above

---

[1] Tac. *Hist.* 5.12.
[2] Tac. *Hist.* 5.3–4.
[3] Plin. *HN* 5.73.
[4] Suet. *Vesp.* 5.6–7; Cass. Dio 65.1.4.
[5] Porph. *Abst.* 4.11–13.

all the vast compendia of rabbinic debates and rulings which began to be compiled around the year 200 as the Mishnah and the Tosefta, and were later expanded in both Palestine and Babylonia as the Talmud, the collections which form much of the basis of modern rabbinic Judaism. Passages of rabbinic literature, especially passages in the Babylonian Talmud which date from the fourth century or later, occasionally include material which closely parallels traditions found in Josephus. For instance, in the *Antiquities* we find the tale of a banquet hosted by the Hasmonaean monarch John Hyrcanus, at which a Pharisee named Eleazar dares to suggest that John should give up the high priesthood on the grounds that his paternity was questionable because his mother had been a prisoner of war. This leads to John switching his allegiance to the Sadducee school and persecuting the Pharisees (*AJ* 13.288–300). The story is repeated in rather similar terms in the Babylonian Talmud but there are striking differences, too: here, the names and sectarian affiliations of the characters are different and the whole thing takes place in the reign not of John Hyrcanus but of his son Alexander Jannaeus.[6] Similarly, the story of Herod's terrible deathbed resolution to massacre the popular leaders of Judaea, mentioned in Chapter 1 above (*BJ* 1.659–69; *AJ* 17.174–9, 193), is retold in the rabbinic corpora, but applied to Alexander Jannaeus instead.[7] We even find mention of an eminent Jewish man who 'defects' from the rebel side to the Roman and wins imperial approval by prophesying Vespasian's accession, although in rabbinic sources the figure involved is not Josephus but Yohanan ben Zakkai, the creator of the first rabbinic 'academy' at Yavneh and the founding father of rabbinic Judaism.[8]

However, there is nothing in any of these parallels which suggests direct knowledge or use of Josephus' texts (although proving intertextuality between different languages is always difficult). The most likely explanation for the parallels is the existence of a 'pool' of (probably oral) legendary material which was common to both Josephus and the editors of the Babylonian Talmud. This would explain the multiple differences of detail, as well as the broad similarity of content.[9] In the case of the Yohanan story, it may be that some version of the Josephus story circulated in the region before later

---

[6] b.Qidd.66a. On this story, see Kalmin 2016: 297–9.
[7] Branch P. scholion on Megillat Ta'anit, Shevat 1–3. On this parallel, see Tropper 2024.
[8] b.Git.56a–b. On Yohanan, see Tropper 2005.
[9] On these parallels, see Cohen 1986; Kalmin 2016; Noam 2017.

coming to be attached to a more popular figure from the period. So, for all these common elements, there is nothing in the rabbinic compilations which suggests that the rabbis were reading Josephus.

The Josephan corpus, then, had a distinctly underwhelming impact in both 'pagan' and Jewish circles. However, one community of Late Antique readers simply could not get enough of his works. Early Christian authors eagerly consumed Josephus' books, and eagerly advertised their great enthusiasm for them and their author. The doctors of the Early Church describe our author as 'almost a second Livy', 'the Greek Livy', 'the most noted of the Jews', 'worthy of credit because of his truthfulness', and 'highly esteemed'.[10] But what lies behind this pervasive early Christian enthusiasm for all things Josephan? Sabrina Inowlocki has identified three principal ways in which Christian authors of Late Antiquity made use of Josephus' texts.[11] First, they provided both arguments and models for Christian apologetic treatises against pagan critiques of the faith (the *Against Apion* was especially important here). Second, they provided support, confirmation, and guidance for biblical exegesis: the *Jewish Antiquities* offered expanded interpretations of many Old Testament narratives, and both the *Antiquities* and the *War* gave additional information on many of the persons mentioned in the Gospels and Acts. Third, and most important of all, the *Jewish War* would prove to be instrumental in constructing and supporting an evolving Christian understanding of the significance of the Roman destruction of Jerusalem in 70 CE.

The destruction of the Temple was important to Christians because it seemed to say something significant about the relationship between God and the Jews and, by extension, between God and the Christians. The understanding developed that the destruction of Jerusalem symbolized God's final abandonment of the 'Old Covenant': specifically, that, as a result of their rejection of Christ and their perceived responsibility for his execution, the Jews had forfeited God's favour, and God had conferred that favour instead on the Christians. This notion, known as Christian supersessionism, is fundamentally anti-Jewish: it conceptualizes Judaism as a dead religion,

---

[10] Cassiod. *Inst.* 50.17.1; Jer. *Ep.* 22.35; Euseb. *Hist. eccl.* 3.9.2; Euseb. *Hist. eccl.* 3.9.3; Jer. *De vir. ill.* 13.

[11] Inowlocki 2016. For a full list of references to Josephus in early Christian literature, see Schreckenberg 1972: 68–105. For cursory discussion of a wide range of early Christian authors on Josephus, see Hardwick 1989.

and presents the Jews as characterized by blindness and permanently stained with the sin of deicide. The value of Josephus to people invested in this ideology is that he, as a Jewish author, agreed with it in one crucial respect, that the destruction of Jerusalem had been a divinely orchestrated punishment of the Jewish people. Of course, Josephus' vision is radically different because of two major divergences from the Christian interpretation: to him, God's punishment was temporary, not permanent, and the 'sin' being punished was the transgressions of the rebels, not the crucifixion.[12] But, despite these vital differences, that core commonality was enough for Josephus' work to be pressed into service as a validation of anti-Jewish Christian theologies.[13]

Eusebius' account of 70, for instance, in the third book of his *Ecclesiastical History*, takes many details from the *Jewish War*, offering a lingering description of the suffering of the Jews within the walls which closely paraphrases (as he admits) content from the fifth and sixth books of Josephus' history (*Hist. eccl.* 3.5–3.10). But at the beginning of the account, Eusebius explicitly presents all these sufferings of the Jews as punishments for the crucifixion and for their supposed persecution of the apostles (3.5.6), and he concludes it with a restatement of his very un-Josephan claim of causation (3.7.8):

> I do not need to add anything about the disaster that overwhelmed the whole nation after the suffering of the Saviour and after the words spoken by the mob of Jews when they sought the pardon of a bandit and a murderer but begged that the Lord of Life should be taken from them, beyond the words of this historian.

To reinforce his point, he changes details from Josephus, a tendency which is especially noticeable when he ignores Josephus' clear statement that the Temple was destroyed on 10 Av and claims, instead, that the destruction happened on Passover, at the same time as the crucifixion forty years earlier (3.5.6). Thus, with dark irony, is Josephus, that redoubtable defender of the Jewish people, pressed into service to support their condemnation. It is hard to disagree with Martin Goodman's view that Josephus 'would have been astonished and horrified at the reinterpretation of his narrative as a divine judgment on his people for rejection of Christ'.[14]

---

[12] See above, pp. 45–7.

[13] On the importance of the coincidence of this aspect of Josephus' vision with the evolving Christian ideology, see Pollard 2015: 75–6.

[14] Goodman 2019: 26. For more on patristic receptions of Josephus, see Schreckenberg 1987; Mason 2003b: 7–24; Kletter 2016: 368–74.

The fourth-century historiographical work *De excidio Hierosolymitano* ('On the Destruction of Jerusalem'), sometimes known as Pseudo-Hegesippus, is a very strong illustration of just how closely Josephus came to be implicated in this evolving Christian anti-Judaism. The text is a Latin adaptation of the *Jewish War*, although the extent to which the author rewrites, restructures, abbreviates, and rearranges his principal source means that it should be seen as an original work rather than as a 'translation'. For four books, Pseudo-Hegesippus follows the basic structure of Josephus' narrative; then, in Book 5, it radically compresses the last three books of the *War* into one enormous volume. The *War* is clearly not the only text which the author has been reading. Pseudo-Hegesippus was a fan of the Latin classics, creating many allusions to Tacitus, Virgil, Horace, and above all Sallust, but also incorporating material from Christian sources, such as the long digression on Simon Magus based on the *Acts of Peter*, and from the *Jewish Antiquities*.[15] Vital episodes from Josephus, including the prophecy to Vespasian and the Flavian triumph, are omitted. The narrative ends at the fall of Masada, which, as Carson Bay has noted, is figured as the end of Jewish history.[16] In noisy editorial interventions, the author is not afraid of inelegantly hammering his theological framework home (Pseudo-Hegesippus 5.2):

And indeed what was it other than sacrilege, when they extended irreverent hands against the source of their salvation, when they stoned him, when they scourged him, when they seized him, when they killed him? Then truly the divine fire consumed their sacred things. For when they were burned by the Babylonians they were afterwards renewed, destroyed by Pompey they were restored again, but they were thoroughly burned when Jesus came, broken up by the heat of the divine spirit they vanished.[17]

Thus Pseudo-Hegesippus furnishes us with a classicizing and Christianizing Latin adaptation of the *Jewish War*, which strongly insists on 70 CE as a punishment for the crucifixion, which imagines the Jewish Revolt as the end of Judaism, and which even goes so far as to lambast Josephus for failing, in his 'perfidy', to understand the true reason for the momentous events he relates.[18]

---

[15] On the sources and models of Pseudo-Hegesippus, see Bay 2022: 336–74. On the text's pronounced Sallustianism, see Stover and Woudhuysen 2022. For Simon Magus, see Pseudo-Hegesippus 3.2; for the *Antiquities*, see the text's somewhat anti-Josephan adaptation of the *Testimonium Flavianum* at Pseudo-Hegesippus 2.12.

[16] Bay 2021.

[17] Trans. W. Blocker, at https://www.tertullian.org/fathers/hegesippus_05_book5.htm.

[18] See the Book 1 Prologue for explicit denunciation of Josephus' perfidy.

Nor was Pseudo-Hegesippus the only Latin Josephus available. We also possess a much closer Latin rendition of the *Jewish War*, sometimes wrongly attributed to Rufinus, probably undatable but certainly in existence by the ninth century. Cassiodorus, the sixth-century scholar and statesman, records commissioning some 'friends' to translate the twenty-two books of the *Antiquities*. This translation survives (it is actually a translation of both the *Antiquities* and *Against Apion*).[19] Thus, by the end of Antiquity, all of Josephus' books except the *Life* existed in Christian Latin translations, the versions in which they would principally circulate in medieval western Europe.

From antiquity to modernity

In the Byzantine world, Josephus' original Greek texts would continue to be widely copied and influential.[20] Sometime between the ninth and fifteenth centuries, the Byzantine-transmitted Greek text of the *Jewish War* was translated and reworked into an important, if somewhat wayward, Slavonic version.[21] Similarly, Josephus (or the Hebrew *Yosippon*, which, as we will soon see, derives substantially from Josephus) was translated into Arabic versions, allowing the Josephan tradition to enter both Islamic and Jewish historiography in that language. The Islamic reception of Josephus needs more scholarly attention, but there is clearly a story there to tell. In the fourteenth century, the great Muslim historian Ibn Khaldūn recalled reading, in Egypt, a book on the history of the Jews from the Maccabees to 70 CE, written by one Yūsuf ibn Kuryūn, an eminent Jewish man who fought the Romans, was captured by Vespasian, and was present with Titus when Jerusalem fell.[22]

In the world of Western Christianity, Josephus' works primarily circulated in those Late Antique Latin versions, elevated by the praises of the Church Fathers and wedded to anti-Jewish theological notions, which their author would neither have recognized nor endorsed. Josephus seems to have been extremely popular in western Europe throughout the medieval period. More than 230 manuscripts of the

---

[19] On these Latin versions, see Levenson and Martin 2016.
[20] On Josephus in Byzantium, see Bowman 1987.
[21] On the Slavonic *Jewish War*, see Leeming 2016.
[22] Fischel 1961: 114–16.

Latin Josephus survive, making him easily one of the most widely copied ancient authors in the medieval world.[23] His influence was strongly felt in the rarified atmospheres of monastic and scholastic communities, and his works were known and used by such luminaries as Bede, William of Malmesbury, and Isidore of Seville.[24] Just as significantly, we have ample testimony of more popular forms of reception too. Instrumental to these was the anonymous Latin prose work known as the *Vindicta salvatoris* ('The Avenging of the Saviour'), the earliest manuscripts of which date to Flanders in the ninth century, and which is also preserved in many later variants from across Europe.[25] The work demonstrates no direct familiarity with Josephus, but it certainly engages with the broader tradition of Josephan reception, featuring as it does a virulent strain of anti-Judaism and a clear interest in presenting 70 CE as God's punishment for the crucifixion. It is an altogether odd composition, riddled with geographical and historical errors, which presents Titus and Vespasian as 'sub-kings' under the emperor Tiberius who convert to Christianity and set out to destroy Jerusalem consciously as avengers of Jesus Christ. In the *Vindicta*, the Flavians become Christian proto-crusaders who deliberately plan to exterminate Judaism in revenge for the supposed deicide carried out by the Jewish people.

The *Vindicta* would be widely influential, spawning a whole series of anti-Jewish romances on the theme of 70, as well as a pan-European theatrical tradition of spectacular dramas depicting the fall of Jerusalem.[26] Later medieval texts based on the *Vindicta* which demonstrate some familiarity with Josephus also appeared, most famously the thirteenth-century French *chanson de geste La destruction de Jérusalem* and the fourteenth-century Middle English alliterative poem *The Siege of Jerusalem*. These works 'correct' some of the *Vindicta*'s errors and incorporate Josephan material: *The Siege of Jerusalem*, for instance, includes passages on the cannibalism of Maria (lines 1081–96) and on Vespasian's conduct of the Roman civil war of 69 CE (897–964) which must have ultimately originated in

---

[23] Levenson and Martin 2016: 322–3.
[24] Pollard 2015; Kletter 2016.
[25] Hall 2016: 41–2.
[26] On the theatrical tradition, see Wright 1989. For Josephan reception in later theatrical history, see Auger 2016.

a Latin version of the *Jewish War*, combining the core narrative of the *Vindicta* with Josephan content.[27]

Receptions such as these would have had a much broader audience than just scholars and clerics, and fed into popular attitudes which had lamentable real-world consequences. In 1190, the Jews of York were besieged in York Castle by a Christian mob led by a crusading knight, and their appeals to the authorities brought no relief. The tragic result was the collective suicide of every person in the castle, and thus the destruction of the city's entire Jewish community. The contemporary Christian historian William of Newburgh wrote a famous account of these terrible events which was clearly modelled on Josephus' Masada narrative, with the rabbi Yom Tov, who died in the castle, given a speech which is reminiscent of Josephus' oration of Eleazar ben Yair. William concludes his account with the following observation:

> Such irrational madness turned by rational people against themselves is a thing to be wondered at. But anyone who has read the history of Josephus concerning the Jewish war will readily appreciate that this type of insane conduct, to which the Jews are prone whenever unfortunate events happen to befall them, has persisted into our times from their ancient superstition.[28]

Thus was Josephus called upon to explain the consequences of the virulent Christian anti-Judaism which his own works had been made to corroborate.[29]

In the tenth century, (probably) in Naples, Josephus finally re-entered Jewish literature, albeit indirectly. An anonymous Hebrew author created a remarkable work known as *Sefer Yosippon* ('the Book of Yosef'), which drew on the Latin versions of Josephus as its principal sources, but reworked them extensively and spliced in material from elsewhere, creating a text which is clearly heavily dependent on Josephus and yet equally clearly something original and new.[30] The work begins by updating the biblical Table of Nations (Genesis 10) to explain the origins of the peoples known to the author. Its second chapter is a remarkable melange of Virgil, Livy, and Jewish legends, describing the early history of Italy, including the tale of how Esau's

---

[27] On the *Siege of Jerusalem*, see B. Millar 2000; Pareles 2023: 4–5.
[28] William of Newburgh, *History of England*, 4.10.
[29] On William's Josephan narrative, see Nisse 2017: 22–3; Vincent 2013.
[30] Hebrew edition: Flusser 1978–80. English translation: Bowman 2023. For an overview, see Dönitz 2016; Goodman 2019: 31–5.

son Zepho came to Hesperia with Aeneas and later became Janus-Saturn, the first god-king of Latium.[31] After these arresting prolegomena, the text begins relating Jewish history from the time of Daniel down to Masada. Initially, it draws primarily on Josephus' *Antiquities*, but the story of the Great Revolt mostly derives from Pseudo-Hegesippus.

What is particularly noticeable, though not surprising, about its handling of Pseudo-Hegesippus is how it skilfully and completely eradicates any trace of that text's Christian supersessionism. The idea that 70 was the Jews' punishment for killing Christ is wholly excised and (as in Josephus) the destruction is instead explained as a punishment for the transgressions of the Jewish rebels. The Masada episode, which ends the text, is reworked significantly: now, instead of committing collective suicide, the warriors on the rock launch what they know will be a doomed final assault against the Romans and die in battle (*Sefer Yosippon* 89). Future-oriented content is added to the Masada story too (89):

May it be the will of God our Lord that he remember the oath of our ancestors. May he rebuild our city, and may he renew our Temple. May he gather our dispersed and collect our banished and return our captives. May he hasten our messiah and hurry our redemption. May he cause our enemies to fall and humble those who hate us.[32]

As we have seen, Pseudo-Hegesippus made Masada the end of Jewish history. By additions such as these, the author of *Yosippon* makes it very clear that this is not the case.

It is in this heavily adapted version that 'Josephus' would primarily be encountered by Jewish readers for most of the next millennium, in the Latin West, the Greek East, and beyond.[33] This would only begin to change in the nineteenth century, when the advent of the academic movement known as *Wissenschaft des Judentums* ('scientific study of Judaism') would inspire greater interest in the Greek texts and stimulate Hebrew and Yiddish translations of Josephus' original works.[34]

---

[31] On Zepho, see Bowman 2019: 57–8.
[32] Translation from Bowman 2023.
[33] On the Jewish reception of *Yosippon*, see Dönitz 2015; Goodman 2019: 33–5.
[34] *Wissenschaft des Judentums* largely amounted to the application to ancient Jewish material of the forms of philological and source-critical scholarship which prevailed in contemporary classics. For *Wissenschaft* more broadly, see Goodman 2018: 447, 462–3. For its impact on receptions of Josephus, see Goodman 2019: 88–94.

The 'rediscovery' of Greek learning in western Europe in the fifteenth century brought Josephus' Greek texts back into circulation, and at the same time the spread of mechanized printing expanded the reach of his works. Peter Burke has surveyed printed editions of classical historians between 1450 and 1700 with the aim of discovering their relative 'popularity', measured by the number of different printings.[35] Josephus is, across this long period, consistently the most 'popular' Greek-language historian. The seventy-three editions of the *Antiquities* and the sixty-eight editions of the *War* are almost double the number of printings of authors whom we might expect to be more widely read, Herodotus (forty-four) and Thucydides (forty-one). Burke also notes the popularity of vernacular translations of Josephus, second only to Tacitus among the authors surveyed.[36] One possible reason for the popularity of the vernacular *Antiquities* may have been the dubious legal status in this period of translations of the bible. Translations of the *Antiquities* were a way in which people could experience biblical stories in their own language without risking censure or punishment.[37]

It was during this period of early printed versions of Josephus that the passage of our author which is perhaps most famous nowadays first came to prominence in religious polemics. The *Testimonium Flavianum* is a short passage from the eighteenth book of the *Jewish Antiquities* which mentions the crucifixion of Jesus, and which also attributes to him great miracles and messianic status.[38] No Josephus scholar working today believes that the text of the *Testimonium* as we currently have it actually goes back to Josephus; however, some have concluded that, though the passage has been doctored by Christian copyists, it is probably based on a brief note on Jesus which originates with Josephus.[39] The *Testimonium* was noticed by early Christians, of course, but it really came to prominence in the Italian Renaissance, initially in the works of the Christian humanist scholars Marsilio Ficino (1433–99) and Bartolomeo Platina (1421–81). From their time on, the passage was often cited as a Jewish witness to the divinity of Christ.[40]

---

[35] Burke 1966.
[36] Burke 1966: 138.
[37] Castelli 2016: 408–9.
[38] *AJ* 18.63–4. On the *Testimonium* more broadly, see Whealey 2003, 2016.
[39] On the modern controversy, see Whealey 2003: 165–201.
[40] Kokin 2016. See also Castelli 2016.

By the early eighteenth century, Josephus' texts were sufficiently familiar for authors to include complex allusions to them which expected knowledge of the originals on the part of readers.[41] Familiarity was greatly facilitated by the proliferation of vernacular translations, which were made into many European languages from the fifteenth century on. Gohei Hata (more on whom shortly) has catalogued all known English versions between 1602 and 1912, and found no fewer than twelve different translations, some with multiple editions.[42] Despite all this competition, one version came unquestionably to be the most successful of all the English Josephuses. In 1737, William Whiston published his monumental translation of the complete works. A one-time professor of mathematics at Cambridge who lost his chair because of his eccentric religious opinions, Whiston devoted much of his enforced early retirement to this work. The result is not fully satisfactory as a translation, but for all its flaws it is easy to understand why Whiston came to enjoy such a wide readership. His English style is fluent, expressive, and highly readable even today.

Whiston's edition would be a runaway success: so many different printings of his translation were carried by so many presses across the Anglophone world that it may indeed be impossible to determine just how many editions existed.[43] Throughout the later eighteenth and nineteenth century, Whiston became an essential companion to the bible, a presence in a great many English-speaking homes, even among the relatively humble. Fuelled by Whiston's success, references to Josephus appear in the works of significant authors of the era: Mark Twain, Thomas Hardy, and Rudyard Kipling.[44] Whiston's great success may have ushered in the historical high-water mark of Josephan popularity in Anglophone countries. For good and ill, Whiston is still very much with us, as the most easily accessible free English version of Josephus' works online.

---

[41] See, for instance, the complex Josephan allusions in Defoe's fictionalized *Journal of a Plague Year* (Nicholson 1919: 14–16), or Jonathan Swift alluding to the *Jewish War*, the source of one of the archetypal myths of infant cannibalism, in a treatise which satirically suggests that the babies of the poor should be sold as food to the rich as a solution to poverty in Ireland (Swift 2018: 156–7).
[42] Hata 2016.
[43] Goodman 2019: 84–6.
[44] For the references to these authors, see Goodman 2019: 86–7; on Whiston more broadly, Goodman 2019: 84–7.

'Masada shall not fall again': Josephus in the twentieth century

Highly significant events of the 1930s and 1940s – the rise of Nazism, the Holocaust in Europe, and the foundation of the state of Israel in the Middle East – created new priorities in twentieth-century Josephan receptions. We will begin in Europe. After a promising early career, the Jewish novelist and playwright Lion Feuchtwanger was, in 1933, stripped of his German citizenship by the new Nazi administration and forced to relocate, first to France and then to Los Angeles. It was during this unsettled period, between 1932 and 1942, that he would produce an important trilogy of historical novels featuring Josephus as protagonist, and chronicling the life of the historian from his embassy to Nero to his (imagined) ignominious death on a Galilean hillside.[45] Feuchtwanger's Josephus is a memorable protagonist, alternating between delusional self-assurance and bouts of paralysing self-doubt, torn between the ardent Jewish 'nationalism' of his youth and his later ambitions to become a cosmopolitan 'citizen of the world'.

The first book focuses on the period of the Jewish Revolt itself, as Josephus drifts from ardent anti-colonial passion to nascent cosmopolitanism. By its close, Josephus' malady is appreciated by Tiberius Julius Alexander, a Jewish apostate and Roman imperial administrator who accompanies Titus to Jerusalem: 'This man Josephus wants to have it all, both Judaism and Hellenism. That is not possible, dear fellow. Jerusalem and Rome, Isaiah and Epicurus: these things cannot be reconciled. We must choose one over the other.'[46] The second book depicts Josephus as a successful author in Rome following the publication of the *Jewish War*, and concentrates on his attempts to raise his two sons: one, raised in Judaism, is killed by a malicious prank of his Gentile playmates; the other, raised Greek, casts off all attachments to Judaism and goes to Judaea with the Roman army. The final book depicts the reign of Domitian, 'master and god', who sees himself as the enemy of the Jewish God, and whose rise to power is accompanied by widespread violence against Jews, in scenes likely to remind Feuchtwanger's readers of the rise of fascism in Germany. Finally, our hero returns to his homeland and abandons his cosmopolitan ideals completely. When revolt begins stirring once

---

[45] All three volumes in the original German are conveniently collected in Feuchtwanger 2013. English translations are also available: Feuchtwanger 1932, 1936, and 1942.
[46] Feuchtwanger 2013: 337.

again under Trajan, he throws himself into it with the same spirit as he had as a young man, and ends up killed by soldiers under the command of his estranged Roman son Paulus.

Feuchtwanger's Josephus trilogy is a stunning achievement of historical imagination, but also a somewhat dispiriting read, particularly when its context is remembered. The author finds in Josephus echoes of the mid-twentieth-century European Jewish experience, explicating the agonies of recent history through this vivid figure from antiquity. The books raise questions concerning the difficulty of maintaining a colonially hyphenated identity, especially when different parts of that identity seem to be pulling in different directions; they also illuminate the dangers of living as part of a minority, perpetually dependent on the goodwill and 'tolerance' of a fickle majority. Above all, in Josephus' final rejection of his quest to become a Greek–Roman–Jew, the trilogy speaks to the tragic failure of the optimistic cosmopolitanism which characterized liberal German circles prior to the rise of Nazism.

In the Middle East, Josephan receptions have focused on the Masada episode. Reverence for Josephus' Masada narrative predated the foundation of the state of Israel. In 1920, during the British Mandate, the Ukrainian poet Yitzhak Lamdan immigrated to the region and would subsequently publish *Masada*, a Hebrew epic poem which engages with the Josephan account (possibly via *Sefer Yosippon*) while celebrating the stories of those early immigrants, drawn to the ancestral land by the promise of imminent nationhood.[47] Lamdan uses the word 'Masada' not to denote the rock itself but as a metonym for the entire envisioned state, proudly defended but hemmed in by perceived enemies. Modern readers have detected deep ambivalences in his reception of Josephus' account (perhaps mirroring the ambivalences in Josephus' own tonally elusive presentation of the siege), and a concern that Israel could become a trap, rather than a sanctuary, for the Jewish people.[48] Even the poem's most famous line, 'Masada shall not fall again', which would have a long afterlife as an Israeli patriotic slogan, reflects ambivalence: note that it does not present the defenders of Masada as heroes, but rather as a negative *exemplum* whose behaviour must not be imitated. But the subsequent reception of this poem in Israel would largely be deaf to these ambiguities and reservations: it

---

[47] On *Sefer Yosippon*, see Y. Feldman 2009.
[48] On the ambivalences, see B. Schwartz et al. 1986: 155–8; Ben-Yehuda 1995: 220–3; Y. Feldman 2009.

became a foundational document for nationalists and an essential set text in schools.[49] Lamdan laid the foundations for Masada's future status as a secular pilgrimage site in a land otherwise full of actual pilgrimage sites.

It was in the 1960s that the 'Masada myth' truly took off. Building on exploratory surveys by earlier visitors such as Shmaryahu Guttman, the eminent Israeli archaeologist and former Chief of Staff of the Israel Defence Forces (IDF) Professor Yigael Yadin oversaw extensive excavations of the plateau between 1963 and 1965.[50] A gifted communicator, Yadin's media appearances helped to transform his excavations into a global sensation, attracting volunteers from around the world, all assisted by logistical support from the IDF. In 1966, Yadin published a lavishly illustrated book presenting his findings to a general audience, entitled in its English edition *Masada. Herod's Fortress and the Zealots' Last Stand*. The presentation of the finds to a non-specialist readership is exemplary; their interpretation is sometimes less so. Yadin seems driven to use the material evidence to 'support' his reading of the mass suicide of the Masada defenders in *Jewish War* 7. Indeed, close to the beginning he revealingly writes 'It would be one of the tasks of our archaeological expedition to see what evidence we could find to support the Josephus record.'[51]

Yadin often seems eager to explain away discrepancies between the material remains and Josephus' account.[52] He can also offer somewhat tenuous interpretations, seemingly in order to validate elements of Josephus' story. For instance, he suggests that the twelve ostraca bearing Hebrew names which were found in one part of the Northern Palace may be the remains of the ten lots which were drawn as part of the suicide pact in Josephus' narrative, despite numerous possible objections (not least that there were twelve of them, rather than ten).[53] As Nachman Ben-Yehuda has discussed, Yadin publicly presented the partial remains of three individuals found on the lower terrace of the Northern Palace as a 'zealot' commander and his wife and child, despite the fact that documented discussions between the

---

[49] Ben-Yehuda 1995: 222–3.
[50] For the contributions of Guttman, see Ben-Yehuda 1995: 50–3; Goodman 2019: 127–9.
[51] Yadin 1966: 15.
[52] See, for example, Magness 2019: 192 on Yadin's explanation for the evident fire damage to the storage areas, contradicting Josephus' statement that the rebels left their provisions untouched at the time of their suicide.
[53] Yadin 1966: 197–201. See also Magness 2019: 195.

excavators had previously established that the three people could not have been a family unit.⁵⁴ And even his reading of Josephus seems partial. Note how, in the book's title and throughout, Yadin refers to the defenders of Masada as 'zealots', despite Josephus' consistent identification of them as *sicarii*. Was Yadin attempting to associate the defenders with a Jewish rebel faction who were rather easier to admire than the *sicarii*, portrayed in Josephus as problematic 'terrorists'?

Yadin's excavations, and his somewhat sensationalist publication of them, had a strong effect, and the tale of Masada, as derived from (an Israeli nationalist reading of) Josephus' work, came to be widely disseminated and celebrated in various areas of Israeli life. School trips to the site became all but mandatory; the IDF swore in members of the armoured divisions on the plateau until 1991; visiting US presidents were given tours of the site.⁵⁵ Thus a narrative written by Josephus came to be central to the self-image and national consciousness of a modern state. But much time has passed since the publication of Yadin's archaeological blockbuster, and it has come under attack from several directions. Archaeologists have queried his interpretations of material evidence; historians and literary scholars have problematized his heroic reading of Josephus; and modern sociologists have investigated the undesirable effects of the 'Masada complex' on contemporary Israel.⁵⁶ However, unlike the 960 *sicarii*, the 'Masada myth' does not die easily. Visitors who take the cable car up to the site are still treated to a ten-minute informational video which relates Yadin's preferred heroic reading of the Josephan narrative, all enlivened by footage from the 1981 American television miniseries *Masada*, which was filmed on-site and features the great Peter O'Toole as Flavius Silva.

The use of the Masada narrative by the Israeli right has, in turn, prompted dissident readings of that episode. In 2005, the Israeli documentarian Avi Mograbi premiered his film *Avenge but One of My Two Eyes*, which engages closely with the modern legacy of Josephus' Masada episode. The film is structured around a telephone conversation between Mograbi and a Palestinian friend, but the discussion is intercut with scenes from contemporary Israel and

---

⁵⁴ Ben-Yehuda 1995: 67–8.
⁵⁵ On school trips, see Ben-Yehuda 1996: 163–78; on the IDF, see Ben-Yehuda 1996: 147–62; on presidential visits, see Magness 2019: 198–9.
⁵⁶ Archaeologists: Magness 2019. Historians and literary scholars: Vidal-Naquet 1978; Cohen 1982b; Ladouceur 1987; Chapman 2007b. Sociologists: B. Schwartz et al. 1986; Ben-Yehuda 1996.

Palestine which suggest startling and uncomfortable parallels between ancient and modern. We see scenes of Palestinian civilians being treated humiliatingly by soldiers; we also follow groups of religious tourists being shown around the Masada site, and watch as they are given the heroic version of Josephus' story, including a dramatic reading of Eleazar's speech. The film juxtaposes the Israeli right's veneration of ancient martyrs, those who preferred death to oppression under occupation, with its unwillingness to concede that similar motivations may animate Palestinian militants. It works largely through striking parallels. As Mograbi's friend passionately discourses on how Israel has made death preferable to life for Palestinians, he seems to become a modern-day Eleazar; similarly, the Israeli soldiers become Romans, a particularly provocative comparison, given the IDF's use of Masada for military ceremonial. Mograbi's documentary suggests that, far from being the sole property of Israeli nationalists, Josephus' Masada narrative has broad resonance. It accuses Josephus' account of contributing to the dehumanization of Palestinians which is evident in some parts of Israeli society, but it simultaneously suggests that the 'Masada myth' contains within it the potential to elicit something which can be in short supply: Israeli empathy for Palestinian suffering.

The potentially broad resonance of the *Jewish War* is also illustrated by its Japanese translation by the distinguished classicist and biblical scholar Gohei Hata, completed when Hata returned to Japan after obtaining his PhD in Philadelphia in 1985. In a talk on his career given at Clare Hall, Cambridge in 2013, Prof. Hata recalls an interesting detail about his experience:

> As soon as I returned to Japan from America, a publisher in Tokyo gave me a chance to translate the works of Josephus from Greek into Japanese. I presume my publisher had already read Josephus in English translation. He showed me his keen interest in Josephus because of his past experiences in the [Second] World War…He was thinking about reasons why Japan – such a small country, like the country of the Jewish people – fought against America, which could be likened to the Roman Empire. He was also trying to explain the appearance of military fanaticism by comparing it with the fanaticism of the zealots described fully in the *Jewish War*.[57]

Prof. Hata leaves the final compelling parallel unspoken: both conflicts ended with spectacular acts of violent destruction which transformed the societies in question, at Hiroshima and Nagasaki as much as at

---

[57] Hata 2013.

Jerusalem. Hata (or at least his publisher) thus sees in Josephus a text which carries lessons for his own people, and for interpreting the traumas of recent history.

Gohei Hata's Japanese Josephus and Avi Mograbi's Palestinian Masada suggest that, although the *Jewish War* may have particular resonance for Jewish readers, it also has the power to speak to any national, ethnic, or religious community grappling with legacies of collective trauma. When Feuchtwanger, Lamdan, Yadin, Mograbi, and Hata reach back to this ancient text to illuminate contemporary concerns, they are following the example of the author of that ancient text, who read the trauma of the fall of the Second Temple in the light of the biblical accounts of the fall of the First, a layered demonstration of the therapeutic potential of historiography.

A Josephus for our times

Josephus continues to be a useful tool to think with today. I will complete this survey of Josephan receptions by focusing on two early twenty-first-century novels which engage closely with his works, and consider how those works are being used in the present.

In 2011 *The Dovekeepers* was published, a historical novel by the American author Alice Hoffman, which relates the tale of the fall of Masada in ways which are clearly informed by Josephus' narrative, but which also represent a strikingly different perspective from that of the historian. Josephus mentions that there were women and children on the rock at the time of the siege: he informs us that some of the *sicarii* had brought their families with them (*BJ* 7.321). However, he tells us almost nothing about them. The only times they are prominent in the narrative are when they are being massacred by their menfolk (*BJ* 7.389–400) and at the very end, when female voices finally emerge as witnesses in the two women and five children who escaped the mass suicide by hiding in a cistern (*BJ* 7.399). Again, Josephus tells us nothing about them at all, not even their names, other than to inform us, helpfully, that one of the two adults was unusually intelligent for a woman.

Hoffman gives these women names: Revka, the baker's wife, and Yael, daughter of a notorious sicarian assassin. These two women each narrate a section of the novel, as do two other characters, Shirah, a 'witch' from Alexandria, and her child, who was raised female but later took the male name Aziza and fought alongside the *sicarii* warriors. We learn their histories and their motivations for retreating to the desert, and with them we experience the Roman occupation, the Revolt, life on the rock, and the final terrifying apocalypse, witnessing a Josephan narrative through a series of un-Josephan viewpoints.

Neither Romans nor *sicarii* emerge from this work with much credit. Hoffman is unsparing in her depictions of the brutalities of the occupation, from the anarchy and terror of the siege and fall of Jerusalem to a particularly shocking scene where a group of deserters from the Tenth Legion torture, rape, and kill Revka's daughter in the wilderness.[58] But the *sicarii* seem little better, often taciturn, cruel, and capable only of devotion to their cause. Through the eyes of Aziza, we are shown the extreme brutalities which these bandit raiders inflict on Jewish communities close to their stronghold.[59] By re-narrating Josephus through such radically altered perspectives, Hoffman creates a Masada for the twenty-first century, which amplifies silenced and ignored voices, and which depicts a world in which neither the crass brutalities of colonialism nor the terrifying certainties of religious or nationalist extremism seem like appealing alternatives.

The British novelist Naomi Alderman published *The Liars' Gospel* in 2012. The work presents four alternatives to the New Testament Gospels, tales of the life of Jesus told from the perspectives of Miryam (the Virgin Mary), Iehuda (Judas), Caiaphas, and Bar-Avo (Barabbas). The Gospels are, predictably enough, very important intertexts for this work, but so too are the works of Josephus, especially the *Jewish War*. Josephan material is important throughout, as Alderman narrates numerous episodes related by the historian, but the voice of Josephus seems especially present in the portion of the work that centres on Caiaphas, the high priest who presided over Jesus' trial and the son-in-law of Annas, the most powerful man in Jerusalem. What is striking about the Caiaphas section is just how small a part of it is constituted by the trial of Jesus: Caiaphas spends most of his 'gospel' focused on more important affairs, principally Pontius Pilate's incendiary demand that the Temple should furnish him with money for the construction of an aqueduct (an episode related by Josephus: *BJ* 2.175–7; *AJ* 18.60–2), and his concerns about his wife's infidelity.

---

[58] Hoffman 2011: 12–14, 195–203.
[59] Hoffman 2011: 396–400.

The depiction of Caiaphas in the novel is extraordinarily sympathetic, much more so than many representations of this figure.[60] He is not depicted as a soulless legalist or as a careerist villain. His highest goal throughout is the maintenance of peace with Rome for essentially pious reasons: war would disrupt the offering of the sacrifices as mandated by Torah, and therefore all steps must be taken to avoid conflict. In *The Liars' Gospel*, the Jewish leadership, so often vilified in Christian representations, are reasonable, wise, and correct in their assessment of the situation. On her website, Alderman explains that, as someone who was raised Orthodox Jewish, she grew up self-identifying as a Pharisee, following the traditional identification of the Pharisees as the forerunners of the rabbis. Thus, she found herself alienated by hostile Christian representations of the Pharisees, and of the Jewish leadership of the time (which she identifies with the Pharisees).[61] Through Josephus, another self-identifying Pharisee, Alderman finds the means to construct a kinder reading of these figures which casts the perceived intellectual ancestors of modern Judaism in a more compassionate light. And here one is surely struck by the malleability of Josephan receptions. The same author, and the same text, used by Christian authors to bolster fundamentally anti-Jewish notions of supersessionism are also used by a Jewish author to redeem the forerunners of modern Judaism from two millennia of Christian contempt. One certainly feels that Josephus would have been happier with the modern usage than the ancient.

Conclusion

Down the centuries, Josephus has been many things. In his own lifetime he was a priest, a rebel, a general, a prophet, a prisoner, a traitor, and an intellectual. But perhaps above all, and relatively consistently across the many phases of his life (albeit in different ways), he was a champion of his people, defending them from outside attack, advocating for their dignity and importance, and remaining steadfast in his commitment to his culture despite his 'betrayal' at Jotapata. Since his death, this already expansive resumé has become even more wide-ranging. As we have seen in this chapter, the works

---

[60] For negative receptions of Caiaphas, see Bond 2004: 9–16; Reinhartz 2011.
[61] https://naomialderman.com/books (accessed 26 February 2024).

of Josephus have been used and abused at many different times, by many different reading communities and for many different purposes, more indeed than this survey has had the space to cover. He has provided Christian readers with material to reinforce the notion that Judaism was a dead religion abandoned by its God; he has also been used by Jewish authors to refute and reject Christian contempt of Judaism. He has been an authoritative source for the history of his people for Jews, Muslims, and Christians alike. From Tel Aviv to Tokyo his historical vision has spoken to the concerns of the modern world, along the way bolstering both Israeli nationalism and advocacy for Palestine. He has adorned both the medieval stage and Hollywood's silver screen, prefigured the anxieties and ambivalences of life for European Jews in the twentieth century, served as a point of reference for major authors in the English canon, and enjoyed a level of consistent popularity which the great majority of ancient authors would envy. In their own quiet way, his works rank among the most broadly influential literary productions of classical antiquity.

But if there is one other thing which Josephus has become, at least in Classics departments in the last hundred years or so, it is a 'minor author', a name to be referenced but not engaged with, a figure to be hurried past with minimal fuss on undergraduate courses in Roman historiography as they rush on their way from Velleius to Tacitus. This minimization of his importance seems to be out of keeping with the large footprint that his works have left on world culture, and looks even more difficult to justify in what purports to be an age of decolonization. Josephus' awkward hyphenated identity, which renders him not straightforwardly 'Greek' or 'Roman', may once have seemed like sufficient reason to keep him off Classical syllabuses. It no longer seems sufficient. If anything, his complex identity should nowadays be a reason for closer and more extensive engagement.

It is easy enough for classicists and ancient historians to lament the lack of 'provincial literatures' from the Roman world. This justifies us maintaining a close, even an exclusive, focus on those authors who have long been considered central to the canon, and who are generally unproblematically Greek or Roman in ways that Josephus is not. But the fact is that provincial literatures are out there, in some quantity: all we need to do is look. Classics will not long be able to escape the charges of Eurocentrism and dead-white-maleism if it cannot find space for this wider world: not just Josephus, but also Philo of Alexandria; Manetho, Berossus, and Philo of Byblos; the

Habakkuk Pesher and the Edicts of Ashoka; the book of Revelation, the Avesta, and the Qur'an; the Egyptian *Lamb's Oracle* and the poetry of Ephrem the Syrian; the hexameters of legionaries from Bu Njem in Libya and the verse epitaphs of Roman Britain. There are literary worlds far beyond the 'canon' that we learn as undergraduates, and perhaps this is what Josephus could be for our subject at this time: an invitation to establish a broader, more inclusive, and richer definition of which texts get to count as 'classics'.

RECOMMENDED READING

Texts, translations, commentaries, and general works

The easiest way to access reliable editions of the Greek texts of Josephus is through the Loeb editions (Thackeray et al. 1926–65), which also provide facing translations. For other translations, readers of the *Jewish War* are fortunate: both Hammond 2017 and Williamson 1981 provide readable English versions. The other texts are a little trickier. In addition to the Loebs, the excellent ongoing series *Flavius Josephus. Translation and Commentary* (series editor Steve Mason) provides highly reliable modern English versions of the texts, as well as indispensable commentaries. The series is not, at the time of writing, complete, but many volumes have been published, and every one of them has made a significant impact on scholarship. Currently available volumes are, in series order, Mason 2008; Mason 2022; L. Feldman 2000; Begg 2004; Begg and Spilsbury 2005; Spilsbury and Seeman 2016; Van Henten 2013; Mason 2001; and Barclay 2006. Other than this, William Whiston's 1737 English translation is widely available online, and the Wordsworth edition of Whiston's *Antiquities* (Whiston 2006) contains a very useful introduction by Brian McGing.

Short overviews of the historian are provided by Chapman 2009 and Price 2011a. Moehring 1984 has been a widely influential survey. Good book-length introductory overviews are provided by Bilde 1988, Rajak 2002, and Mason 2003b. Bilde 1988 is out of print and can be quite difficult to obtain nowadays, but it is worth the effort, above all for its outstanding survey of prior scholarship. Even more generous assistance with older scholarship is provided by Louis Feldman's comprehensive annotated Josephus bibliography (L. Feldman 1984). The concordance of Rengstorf 1968–83 is still highly valuable, even in this age of searchable online text databases. More recently, Chapman and Rodgers 2016 is an outstanding collection of introductory essays to important Josephan topics.

Several important edited volumes on Josephus have been published in the last few decades, offering insights into a miscellaneous array of topics. Notable among them are L. Feldman and Hata 1987; L. Feldman and Hata 1989; Parente and Sievers 1995; Mason

1998c; Edmondson et al. 2005; Sievers and Lembi 2005; Rodgers 2007; and Pastor et al. 2011.

Chapter I

Good overviews of Judaea under Roman rule are provided by S. Schwartz 2001 and Eck 2007. Goodman 2007 offers focused examinations of key aspects of Judaean (and Roman) culture in this period, as well as insights into the causes and consequences of the Jewish Revolt. For the Revolt itself, Mason 2016a is a not-uncontroversial reading. Numerous more conventional narratives (which tend to follow Josephus' interpretative framework much more closely than Mason) are available: Price 1992 and Rogers 2021 are especially recommended. Magness 2012 and Meyers and Chancey 2012 provide nicely written surveys of the material evidence. For Graeco-Roman views of Judaism, see Schäfer 1997 and Isaac 2004.

Chapter II

Mason 2016c provides an excellent, clear and short introduction to the *War*. Mader 2000 has been important in discussion of the work's rhetorical strategies. Davies 2023 gives detailed readings of Josephus' engagement with Rome and (especially) the Flavians. Glas 2024 analyses Josephus' self-presentation in the *War*. Vidal-Naquet 1977, originally the introduction to a French translation of the *War*, is an extraordinary piece of work by one of the twentieth century's leading classical historians, essential reading for anyone engaging with this text.

Chapter III

For introductions to and overviews of the *Antiquities*, see Mason 1998b; D. Schwartz 2016; Mason's introduction to L. Feldman 2000; and Davies in press. L. Feldman 1998a and b are fundamental to modern scholarship. Attridge 1976 remains important for the theology of the *Antiquities*. Westwood 2023 is important for Josephus' Moses. Sterling 1992 is valuable for ancient traditions of apologetic historiography.

Chapter IV

The introduction to Mason 2001 and Mason 2016b provide excellent short introductions to the *Life*. Cohen 1979 in many ways initiated the modern study of the *Life*, and also includes important insights into the *War* and the *Antiquities*. Grojinowksi 2023 reads the work in the light of Graeco-Roman autobiography. Siegert et al. 2001 provides commentary.

Chapter V

For good introductions to the *Against Apion*, see the introduction to Barclay 2006 and Barclay 2016. The former is an outstanding contribution overall, the Platonic ideal of a commentary. Labow 2005 and Siegert 2008 also include extensive notes and commentary. The edited volume by L. Feldman and Levison 1996 contains many valuable considerations of this treatise.

Chapter VI

Goodman 2019 is an exemplary study of the reception history of the *Jewish War*, and Schatz 2019 surveys modern Jewish receptions of Josephus. Both of these volumes were generated by a major Oxford research project on the reception of Josephus; the same project also resulted in a special issue of the *International Journal of the Classical Tradition* (23.3 [2016]), and the creation of the online Josephus Reception Archive (https://josephus.orinst.ox.ac.uk/archive/jra), which contains short discussions of important moments in Josephan reception history. Chapman and Rodgers 2016 includes an extensive section dedicated to reception.

BIBLIOGRAPHY

Alderman, N. 2012. *The Liars' Gospel*. London, Penguin.
Alexander, P. 2021. 'Celsus' Judaism', in J. C. Paget and S. Gathercole (eds.), *Celsus in His World. Philosophy, Polemic and Religion in the Second Century*. Cambridge, Cambridge University Press: 327–59.
Alon, G. 1977. *Jews, Judaism, and the Classical World. Studies in Jewish History in the Times of the Second Temple and Talmud*. Jerusalem, Magnes Press.
Applebaum, A. 2009. '"The Idumaeans" in Josephus' *Jewish War*', *JSJ* 40: 1–22.
Ash, R. 2014. 'Fractured Vision: Josephus and Tacitus on Triumph and Civil War', in J. M. Madsen and R. Rees (eds.), *Roman Rule in Greek and Latin Writing. Double Vision*. Leiden and Boston, MA, Brill: 144–62.
Attridge, H. W. 1976. *The Interpretation of Biblical History in the* Antiquitates Judaicae *of Flavius Josephus*. Missoula, MT, Scholars Press.
Auger, P. 2016. 'Playing Josephus on the English Stage', *International Journal of the Classical Tradition*, 23: 326–32.
Avigad, N. 1983. *Discovering Jerusalem*. Nashville, TN, T. Nelson.
Bar Kokhva, B. 2010. *The Image of the Jews in Greek Literature. The Hellenistic Period*. Berkeley, CA, University of California Press.
Barclay, J. M. G. 2005. 'The Empire Writes Back: Josephan Rhetoric in Flavian Rome', in Edmondson et al. 2005: 315–31.
———. 2006. *Flavius Josephus. Translation and Commentary Vol. 10. Against Apion*. Leiden, Brill.
———. 2009. 'Josephus' *Contra Apionem* as Jewish Apologetics', in A. Jacobsen, J. Ulrich, and D. Brakke (eds.), *Critique and Apologetics. Jews, Christians and Pagans in Antiquity*. Frankfurt, Peter Lang: 265–82.
———. 2016. '*Against Apion*', in Chapman and Rodgers 2016: 75–85.
Barish, D. A. 1978. 'The "Autobiography" of Josephus and the Hypothesis of a Second Edition of His *Antiquities*', *HThR* 71: 61–75.
Barnes, T. D. 2005. 'The Sack of the Temple in Josephus and Tacitus', in Edmondson et al. 2005: 130–44.
Batey, R. 1991. *Jesus and the Forgotten City. New Light on Sepphoris and the Urban World of Jesus*. Grand Rapids, MI, Baker.
Baumgarten, A. I. 2016. 'Josephus and the Jewish Sects', in Chapman and Rodgers 2016: 261–72.

Bay, C. 2021. 'Writing the Jews out of History: Pseudo-Hegesippus, Classical Historiography, and the Codification of Christian Anti-Judaism in Late Antiquity', *ChHist* 90: 265–85.

———. 2022. *Biblical Heroes and Classical Culture in Christian Late Antiquity. The Historiography, Exemplarity and Anti-Judaism of Pseudo-Hegesippus*. Cambridge, Cambridge University Press.

Beard, W. M. 2003. 'The Triumph of Flavius Josephus', in Boyle and Dominik 2003: 543–58.

Begg, C. T. 1993. *Josephus' Account of the Early Divided Monarchy (AJ 8.212–420). Rewriting the Bible*. Leuven, Peeters.

———. 2004. *Flavius Josephus. Translation and Commentary Vol. 4. Judean Antiquities Books 5–7*. Leiden, Brill.

———. and Spilsbury, P. 2005. *Flavius Josephus. Translation and Commentary Vol. 5. Judean Antiquities Books 8–10*. Leiden, Brill.

Ben-Yehuda, N. 1995. *The Masada Myth. Collective Memory and Mythmaking in Israel*. Madison, WI, University of Wisconsin Press.

Ben Yishai, S. 2021. '"Brigands" and "Tyrants" in Josephus' *Bellum Judaicum*', *CQ* 71: 902–7.

Benaissa, A. 2014. 'P.Oxy. LXXIX 5202: Copy of an Honorific Inscription for the Poetic Victor Apion', *P.Oxy* LXXIX: 125–38.

Berthelot, K. 2003. *Philanthropia judaica. Le débat autour la 'misanthropie' des lois juive dans l'antiquité*. Leiden, Brill.

Bickerman, E. J. 1979. *The God of the Maccabees*. Translated by H. Moehring. Leiden, Brill.

Bilde, P. 1979. 'The Causes of the Jewish War According to Josephus', *JSJ* 10: 179–202.

———. 1988. *Flavius Josephus between Jerusalem and Rome*. Sheffield, JSOT Press.

Birley, A. R. 2000. 'Two Unidentified Senators in Josephus, *A.J.* 19', *CQ* 50: 620–3.

Bloch, R. 2002. *Antike Vorstellungen vom Judentum. Der Judenexcurs des Tacitus im Rahmen der griechisch-römischen Ethnographie*. Stuttgart, Franz Steiner.

———. 2022. *Ancient Jewish Diaspora*. Leiden and Boston, MA, Brill.

Blouin, K. 2005. *Le conflit Judéo-Alexandrin de 38–41. L'identité juive à l'épreuve*. Paris, L'Harmattan.

Bond, H. K. 2004. *Caiaphas. Friend of Rome and Judge of Jesus?* London, John Knox Press.

———. 2012. 'Josephus on Herod's Domestic Intrigue in the *Jewish War*', *JSJ* 43: 295–314.

Bowman, S. 1987. 'Josephus in Byzantium', in Feldman and Hata 1987: 362–85.

———. 2019. '*Sefer Yosippon*: Re-evaluations', *Sefer Yuhasin* 7: 57–64.

———. 2023. *Sepher Yosippon. A Tenth-Century History of Ancient Israel.* Detroit, MI, Wayne State University Press.

Boyle, A. J., and Dominik, W. (eds.) 2003. *Flavian Rome. Culture, Image, Text.* Leiden and Boston, MA, Brill.

Brighton, M. A. 2009. *The Sicarii in Josephus' Judean War. Rhetorical Analysis and Historical Observations.* Atlanta, GA, SBL.

Brunt, P. A. 1979. 'Laus imperii', in P. D. A. Garnsey and C. A. Whittaker (eds.), *Imperialism in the Ancient World.* Cambridge, Cambridge University Press: 159–92.

Burke, P. 1966. 'A Survey of the Popularity of Ancient Historians, 1450–1700', *H&T* 5: 135–52.

Castelli, S. 2016. 'Josephus in Renaissance Italy', in Chapman and Rodgers 2016: 402–13.

Chalmers, M. 2020. 'Viewing Samaritans Jewishly: Josephus, the Samaritans, and the Identification of Israel', *JSJ* 51: 339–66.

Chancey, M. A. 2002. *The Myth of a Gentile Galilee.* Cambridge and New York, Cambridge University Press.

Chapman, H. H. 2005. '"By the Waters of Babylon": Josephus and Greek Poetry', in Sievers and Lembi 2005: 121–46.

———. 2007a. 'Josephus and the Cannibalism of Mary (*BJ* 6.199–219)', in Marincola 2007: 419–26.

———. 2007b. 'Masada in the First and Twenty-First Centuries', in Rodgers 2007: 82–102.

———. 2009. 'Josephus', in Feldherr 2009b: 319–30.

———. and Rodgers, Z. (eds.) 2016. *A Companion to Josephus.* Chichester, Wiley-Blackwell.

Clarke, K. 2011. *Making Time for the Past. Local History and the Polis.* Oxford, Oxford University Press.

Cody, J. M. 2003. 'Conquerors and Conquered on Flavian Coins', in Boyle and Dominik 2003: 105–13.

Cohen, S. J. D. 1979. *Josephus in Galilee and Rome. His* Vita *and Development as a Historian.* Leiden, Brill.

———. 1982a. 'Josephus, Jeremiah, and Polybius', *H&T* 21: 366–81.

———. 1982b. 'Masada: Literary Tradition, Archaeological Remains and the Credibility of Josephus', *Journal of Jewish Studies* 33: 385–405.

———. 1986. 'Parallel Historical Traditions in Josephus and Rabbinic Literature', in *Proceedings of the Ninth World Congress of Jewish Studies 1985, Division B.* Jerusalem, World Union of Jewish Studies: 7–14.

———. 1988. 'History and Historiography in the *Against Apion* of Josephus', *H&T* 27(4): 1–11.

Collins, B. J. (ed.) 2014. *The SBL Handbook of Style.* Second edition. Atlanta, SBL.

Collins, J. J. 2010. *The Scepter and the Star. Messianism in Light of the Dead Sea Scrolls*. Second edition. Grand Rapids, MI, Eerdmans.

Cornell, T. J. 2010. 'Universal History and the Early Roman Historians', in P. Liddel and A. Fear (eds.), *Historiae Mundi. Studies in Universal History*. London, Duckworth: 102–15.

Cotton, H. and Eck, W. 2005. 'Josephus' Roman Audience: Josephus and the Roman Elites', in Edmondson et al. 2005: 37–52.

Cowan, J. A. 2018. 'A Tale of Two *Antiquities*: A Fresh Evaluation of the Relationship Between the Ancient Histories of T. Flavius Josephus and Dionysius of Halicarnassus', *JSJ* 49: 475–97.

Curran, J. 2011. 'Flavius Josephus in Rome', in Pastor et al. 2011: 65–86.

Czajkowski, K. 2015. 'Jewish Attitudes towards the Imperial Cult', *SCI* 34: 181–94.

Czajkowski, K. 2016. 'Justice in Client Kingdoms: The Many Trials of Herod's Sons', *Historia* 65: 473–96.

Czajkowski, K. and Eckhardt, B. 2021. *Herod in History. Nicolaus of Damascus and the Augustan Context*. Oxford, Oxford University Press.

Czajkowski, K. and Friedman, D. A. (eds.) 2024. *Looking In, Looking Out. Jews and Non-Jews in Mutual Contemplation*. Leiden and Boston, MA, Brill.

Damon, C. 2008. '"The mind of an ass and the impudence of a dog": A Scholar Gone Bad', in I. Sluiter and R. Rosen (eds.), *Kakos. Badness and Anti-Value in Classical Antiquity*. Leiden, Brill: 335–64.

———. 2011. 'Pliny on Apion', in R. Gibson and R. Morello (eds.), *Pliny the Elder. Themes and Contexts*. Leiden, Brill: 131–46.

Davies, J. J. S. 2013. '*Divine Justice and Roman Injustice in the Works of Josephus*'. MPhil thesis, University of Oxford.

———. 2019. 'Covenant and Pax Deorum: Polyvalent Prodigies in Josephus' *Jewish War*', *Histos* 13: 78–96.

———. 2020. 'Josephus, Caligula and the Future of Rome', in J. J. Price and K. Berthelot (eds.), *The Future of Rome. Roman, Greek, Jewish and Christian Visions*. Cambridge, Cambridge University Press: 155–68.

———. 2023. *Representing the Dynasty in Flavian Rome. The Case of Josephus'* Jewish War. Oxford, Oxford University Press.

———. 2024. 'Greek Scholarship in Josephus' *Against Apion*', in Czajkowski and Friedman 2024: 124–39.

———. in press. 'Local History as Global Design: Josephus' *Jewish Antiquities*', in D. Miano, J. Thornton, H. Ingelbert, M. Staub, and S. Vidal (eds.), *The Oxford History of Universal History-Writing*. Oxford, Oxford University Press.

Des Places, E. (ed. and trans.) 1973. *Numénius. Fragments*. Paris, Les Belles Lettres.

Dillery, J. 2003. 'Putting Him Back Together Again: Apion Historian, Apion Grammatikos', *CPh* 98: 383–90.
Donaldson, T. L. 1990. 'Rural Bandits, City Mobs and the Zealots', *JSJ* 21: 19–40.
Dönitz, S. 2015. 'Josephus im jiddischen Gewand: die jiddische Übersetzung des *Sefer Yosippon*', *Aschkenas* 25: 53–61.
———. 2016. 'Sefer Yosippon (Josippon)', in Chapman and Rodgers 2016: 382–9.
Dormeyer, D. 2005. 'The Hellenistic Biographical History of King Saul: Josephus, *AJ* 6.45–378 and 1 Samuel 9:1–31:13', in Sievers and Lembi 2005: 147–57.
Drews, R. 1973. *The Greek Accounts of Eastern History*. Cambridge, MA, Harvard University Press.
Eck, W. 2007. *Rom und Judaea*. Tübingen, Mohr Siebeck.
Eckstein, A. M. 1990. 'Josephus and Polybius: A Reconsideration', *ClAnt* 9: 175–208.
Edmondson, J., Mason, S., and Rives, J. (eds.) 2005. *Flavius Josephus in Flavian Rome*. Oxford and New York: Oxford University Press.
Edwards, D. R. 1992. 'Religion, Power and Politics: Jewish Defeats by the Romans in Iconography and Josephus', in J. A. Overman and R. S. Maclennan (eds.), *Diaspora Jews and Judaism. Essays in Honor of, and in Dialogue with, A. Thomas Kraabel*. Atlanta, GA, Scholars Press: 293–310.
———. 2023. 'The Theme of *Stasis* in *Antiquities*: Josephus' Political Philosophy and Periodization of History', in V. Kókai-Nagy and Á. Vér (eds.), *Peace and War in Josephus*. Berlin, De Gruyter: 177–94.
Eshel, H. 2009. *Masada. An Epic Story*. Translated by P. King. Jerusalem, Carta.
Fabry, H.-J. and Scholtissek, K. 2002. *Der Messias. Perspektiven des Alten und Neuen Testaments*. Würzburg, Echter.
Feldherr, A. 2009a. 'Barbarians II: Tacitus' Jews', in Feldherr 2009b: 301–16.
———. (ed.) 2009b. *The Cambridge Companion to the Roman Historians*. Cambridge and New York, Cambridge University Press.
Feldman, L. H. 1984. *Josephus and Modern Scholarship*. Berlin, De Gruyter.
———. 1998a. *Josephus's Interpretation of the Bible*. Berkeley, CA, Los Angeles, CA, and London, University of California Press.
———. 1998b. *Studies in Josephus' Rewritten Bible*. Leiden, Boston, MA, and Cologne, Brill.
———. 2000. *Flavius Josephus. Translation and Commentary Vol. 3. Judean Antiquities 1–4*. Leiden, Brill.

———. and Hata, G. (eds.) 1987. *Josephus, Judaism, and Christianity.* Leiden, Brill.
Feldman, L. H. and Hata, G. (eds.) 1989. *Josephus, the Bible and History.* Leiden, Brill.
Feldman, L. H. and Levison, J. (eds.) 1996. *Josephus' Contra Apionem. Studies in Its Character and Context.* Leiden, Brill.
Feldman, Y. 2009. '"The Final Battle" or "A Burnt Offering"? Lamdan's *Masada* Revisited', *AJS Perspectives* 2009: 30–2.
Ferda, T. 2013. 'Jeremiah 7 and Flavius Josephus on the First Jewish Revolt', *JSJ* 44: 158–73.
Feuchtwanger, L. 1932. *Josephus.* Translated by W. Muir and E. Muir. New York, Viking.
———. 1936. *The Jew of Rome.* Translated by W. Muir and E. Muir. New York, Viking.
———. 1942. *Josephus and the Emperor.* Translated by C. Oram. New York, Viking.
———. 2013. *Josephus-Trilogie. Roman in drei Bänden.* Berlin, Aufbau Verlag.
Fischel, W. J. 1961. 'Ibn Khaldūn's Use of Historical Sources', *Studia Islamica* 14: 109–19.
Flusser, D. 1978–80. *The Josippon.* 2 vols. Jerusalem, Bialik Institute.
Fredriksen, P. 2015. 'If It Looks Like a Duck, and It Quacks Like a Duck...: On *Not* Giving Up the "Godfearers"', in S. A. Harvey, N. P. DesRosiers, S. L. Lander, J. Z. Pastis and D. Ullucci (eds.), *A Most Reliable Witness. Essays in Honor of Ross Shepard Kraemer.* Providence, RI, SBL: 25–33.
Freyne, S. 1980. *Galilee from Alexander the Great to Hadrian, 323 BCE to 135 CE. A Study of Second Temple Judaism.* Wilmington, DE, Michael Glazier.
Gambetti, S. 2009. *The Alexandrian Riots of 38 CE and the Persecution of the Jews. A Historical Reconstruction.* Leiden, Brill.
Gelzer, M. 1964. *Kleine Schriften III.* Wiesbaden, Franz Steiner.
Geva, H. 2014. 'Jerusalem's Population in Antiquity: A Minimalist View', *Tel Aviv* 41: 131–60.
Glas, J. E. 2020. 'Josephus between Jerusalem and Rome: Cultural Brokerage and the Rhetoric of Emotion in the *Bellum Judaicum* (1.9–12)', *Histos* 14: 275–99.
———. 2024. *Flavius Josephus' Self-Characterization in First-Century Rome. A Historiographical Analysis of Autobiographical Discourse in the* Judaean War. Leiden and Boston, MA, Brill.
Gleason, M. 2001. 'Mutilated Messengers: Body Language in Josephus', in S. Goldhill (ed.), *Being Greek under Rome. Cultural Identity, the*

Second Sophistic and the Development of Empire. Cambridge and New York, Cambridge University Press: 50–85.

Gnuse, R. 2002. '*Vita Apologetica*: The Lives of Josephus and Paul in Apologetic Historiography', *Journal for the Study of the Pseudepigrapha* 13: 151–69.

Goodman, M. D. 1987. *The Ruling Class of Judaea. The Origins of the Jewish Revolt against Rome, AD 66–70.* Cambridge, Cambridge University Press.

———. 1994. 'Josephus as a Roman Citizen', in Parente and Sievers 1994: 329–38.

———. 1999. 'Josephus' Treatise *Against Apion*', in M. J. Edwards, M. D. Goodman, and S. R. F. Price (eds.), *Apologetics in the Roman Empire. Pagans, Jews, and Christians.* Oxford, Oxford University Press: 45–58.

———. 2007. *Rome and Jerusalem. The Clash of Ancient Civilisations.* London, Allen Lane.

———. 2018. *A History of Judaism.* Princeton, NJ, Princeton University Press.

———. 2019. *Josephus' Jewish War. A Biography.* NJ, Princeton, Princeton University Press.

Goud, T. E. 1996. 'The Sources of Josephus' *Antiquities* 19', *Historia* 45: 472–82.

Graetz, H. 1888. *Geschichte der Juden von des ältesten Zeiten bis auf die Gegenwart.* Leipzig, O. Leiner.

Grojnowski, D. 2023. *Situating Josephus' Life Within Ancient Autobiography. Genre in Context.* London and New York, Bloomsbury.

Gruen, E. S. 1998. *Heritage and Hellenism. The Reinvention of Jewish Tradition.* Berkeley, CA, University of California Press.

———. 2015. *Diaspora. Jews amidst Greeks and Romans.* Cambridge, MA, Harvard University Press.

———. 2016. *The Construct of Identity in Hellenistic Judaism.* Berlin and Boston, MA, De Gruyter.

Haaland, G. 2007. 'What Difference Does Philosophy Make? The Three Schools as a Rhetorical Device in Josephus', in Rodgers 2007: 262–88.

Hägg, T. 2012. *The Art of Biography in Antiquity.* Cambridge, Cambridge University Press.

Hall, T. N. 2016. 'Nathan the Jew in the Old English *Vindicta Salvatoris*', in S Zacher (ed.), *Imagining the Jew in Anglo-Saxon Literature and Culture.* Toronto, University of Toronto Press.

Hammond, M. 2017. *Josephus. The Jewish War.* Oxford, Oxford University Press.

Hardwick, M. E. 1989. *Josephus as an Historical Source in Patristic Literature through Eusebius.* Atlanta, GA, Scholars Press.

———. 1996. '*Contra Apionem* and Christian Apologetics', in L. Feldman and Levison 1996: 396–402.
Harker, A. 2009. *Loyalty and Dissidence in Roman Egypt. The Case of the Acta Alexandrinorum*. Cambridge, Cambridge University Press.
Hata, G. 1975–6. 'Is the Greek Version of Josephus' *Jewish War* a Translation or a Rewriting of the First Version?', *Jewish Quarterly Review* 66: 89–108.
———. 2013. 'Translating the Greek Bible into Japanese: A Personal History'. University of Cambridge, https://sms.cam.ac.uk/media/1443981 (accessed 7 March 2024).
———. 2016. 'A Note on English Translations of Josephus from Thomas Lodge to D. S. Margoliouth', in Chapman and Rodgers 2016: 414–18.
Haubold, J., Lanfanchi, G. B, Rollinger, R., and Steele, J. (eds.) 2013. *The World of Berossos*. Wiesbaden, Harrassowitz.
Hauken, T. 1998. *Petition and Response. An Epigraphic Study of Petitions to Roman Emperors*. Bergen, Norwegian Institute at Athens.
Hejduk, J. D. 2018. 'Was Vergil Reading the Bible? Original Sin and an Astonishing Acrostic in the *Orpheus and Eurydice*', *Vergilius* 64: 71–102.
Hoffman, A. 2011. *The Dovekeepers*. London, Simon & Schuster.
Hollander, W. den 2014. *Josephus, The Emperors, and the City of Rome*. Leiden and Boston, MA, Brill.
Honigman, S. 2014. 'The Religious Persecution as a Narrative Elaboration of a Military Suppression', in M.-F. Basslet and O. Munnich (eds.), *La mémoire des persécutions. Autour des livres des Maccabées*. Paris, Louvain, and Walpole, MA, Peeters: 59–76.
Horsley, R. 1979. 'Josephus and the Bandits', *JSJ* 10: 37–63.
———. and Hanson, J. 1999. *Bandits, Prophets, and Messiahs. Popular Movements in the Time of Jesus*. Harrisburg, PA, Trinity Press.
Hulls, J.-M. 2018. 'A Last Act of Love? Suicide and Civil War as Tropes in Silius Italicus's *Punica* and Josephus's *Bellum Judaicum*', in L. D. Ginsberg and D. A. Krasne (eds.), *After 69 CE. Writing Civil War in Flavian Rome*. Berlin, De Gruyter: 321–38.
Isaac, B. 2004. *The Invention of Racism in Classical Antiquity*. Princeton, NJ, Princeton University Press.
Inowlocki, S. 2016. 'Josephus and Patristic Literature', in Chapman and Rodgers 2016: 356–67.
Jensen, M. H. 2010. *Herod Antipas in Galilee. The Literary and Archaeological Sources on the Reign of Herod Antipas and Its Socio-Economic Impact on Galilee*. Tübingen, Mohr Siebeck.
Jones, K. R. 2005. 'The Figure of Apion in Josephus' *Contra Apionem*', *JSJ* 36: 278–315.

Kalmin, R. 2016. 'Josephus and Rabbinic Literature', in Chapman and Rodgers 2016: 293–304.

Kaplan, J. 2019. 'Nothing Is True, Everything Is Permitted: Premodern Religious Terrorism', *Terrorism and Political Violence* 31: 1070–95.

Kasher, A. 1988. *Jews, Idumaeans and Ancient Arabs. Relations of the Jews of Eretz Israel with the Nations of the Frontier and the Desert during the Hellenistic and Roman Era (332 BCE – 70 CE)*. Tübingen, Mohr Siebeck.

———. 1996. 'Polemic and Apologetic Methods of Writing in *Contra Apionem*', in L. Feldman and Levison 1996: 143–86.

———. with Witztum, E. 2008. *King Herod. A Persecuted Persecutor*. Berlin and New York, De Gruyter.

Klawans, J. 2012. *Josephus and the Theologies of Ancient Judaism*. Oxford, Oxford University Press.

Kletter, K. M. 2016. 'The Christian Reception of Josephus in Late Antiquity and the Middle Ages', in Chapman and Rodgers 2016: 368–81.

Kneebone, E. 2007. 'Dilemmas of the Diaspora: The Esther Narrative in Josephus, *Antiquities* 11.184–296', *Ramus* 36: 51–77.

Knoppers, G. N. and McConville, J. G. (eds.) 2000. *Reconsidering Israel and Judah. Recent Studies on the Deuteronomistic History*. Philadelphia, PA, Eisenbrauns.

Kokin, D. S. 2016. 'The Josephan Renaissance: Flavius Josephus and His Writings in Italian Humanist Discourse', *Viator* 47: 205–48.

Kokkinos, N. 1998. *The Herodian Dynasty. Origins, Role in Society and Eclipse*. Sheffield, Sheffield Academic Press.

———. 2003. 'Justus, Josephus, Agrippa II and His Coins', *SCI* 22: 163–80.

Kraemer, R. S. 2014. 'Giving Up the God-Fearers', *Journal of Ancient Judaism* 5: 61–87.

Labow, D. (ed. and trans.) 2005. *Flavius Josephus* Contra Apionem *Buch I. Einleitung, Text, Textkritischer Apparat, Übersetzung und Kommentar*. Stuttgart, Kohlhammer.

Ladouceur, D. J. 1987. 'Josephus and Masada', in L. Feldman and Hata 1987: 95–113.

Landau, T. 2006. *Out-Heroding Herod. Josephus, Rhetoric, and the Herod Narratives*. Leiden, Brill.

Laqueur, R. 1920. *Der jüdischer Historiker Flavius Josephus. Ein biographischer Versuch auf neuer quellenkritischer Grundlage*. Giessen, Münchow.

Lavan, M. 2014. 'Slaves to Rome: The Rhetoric of Mastery in Titus' Speech to the Jews (*Bellum Judaicum* 6.328–50)', *Ramus* 36: 25–38.

Leeming, K. 2016. 'The Slavonic Version of Josephus's *Jewish War*', in Chapman and Rodgers 2016: 390–401.

Lenfant, D. 2007. 'Greek Historians of Persia', in Marincola 2007: 183–91.
Leoni, T. 2001. 'Tito e l'incendio del tempio di Gerusalemme: repressione o clemenza disubbidita?', *Ostraka* 9: 455–70.
———. 2007, '"Against Caesar's Wishes": Flavius Josephus as a Source for the Burning of the Temple', *Journal of Jewish Studies* 58: 39–51.
———. 2016. 'The Text of the Josephan Corpus: Principal Greek Manuscripts, Ancient Latin Translations, and the Indirect Tradition', in Chapman and Rodgers 2016: 307–20.
Levenson, D. B. and Martin, T. R. 2016. 'The Ancient Latin Translations of Josephus', in Chapman and Rodgers 2016: 322–44.
Lipschits, O. and Oeming, M. (eds.) 2006. *Judah and the Judeans in the Persian Period*. Philadelphia, PA, Eisenbrauns.
Luce, T. J. 1977. *Livy. The Composition of His History*. Princeton, NJ, Princeton University Press.
Macfarlane, R. T. 1997. 'Hebrew, Aramaic, Greek, and Latin: Languages of New Testament Judaea', *BYU Studies Quarterly* 36: 228–38.
MacRae, G. 1965. 'Miracles in *The Antiquities* of Josephus', in C. F. D. Moule (ed.), *Miracles. Cambridge Studies in Their Philosophy and History*. London, Mowbray: 127–47.
Mader, G. 2000. *Josephus and the Politics of Historiography. Apologetics and Impression Management in the* Bellum Judaicum. Leiden, Brill.
Magness, J. 2012. *The Archaeology of the Holy Land. From the Destruction of Solomon's Temple to the Muslim Conquest*. Cambridge, Cambridge University Press.
———. 2019. *Masada. From Jewish Revolt to Modern Myth*. Princeton, NJ, Princeton University Press.
Maier, J. 1994. 'Amalek in the Writings of Josephus', in Parente and Sievers 1994: 109–26.
Marincola, J. 1997. *Authority and Tradition in Ancient Historiography*. Cambridge, Cambridge University Press.
———. (ed.) 2007. *A Companion to Greek and Roman Historiography*. Oxford and Malden, MA, Blackwell.
Mason, S. 1994. 'Josephus, Daniel, and the Flavian House', in Parente and Sievers 1994: 161–94.
———. 1996. 'The *Contra Apionem* in Social and Literary Context: An Invitation to Judean Philosophy', in L. Feldman and Levison 1996: 187–228.
———. 1998a. 'An Essay in Character: The Aim and Audience of Josephus's *Vita*', in F. Siegert and J. U. Kalms (eds.), *Internationales Josephus-Kolloquium Münster 1997*. Münster, Lit: 31–77.
———. 1998b. '"Should any wish to enquire further": The Aim and Audience of Josephus's *Judean Antiquities*', in Mason 1998c: 64–103.

———. (ed.), 1998c. *Understanding Josephus. Seven Perspectives*. Sheffield, Sheffield Academic Press.

———. 2001. *Flavius Josephus. Translation and Commentary Vol. 9. The Life of Josephus*. Leiden, Boston, MA, and Cologne, Brill.

———. 2003a. 'Flavius Josephus in Flavian Rome: Reading on and between the Lines', in Boyle and Dominik 2003: 559–89.

———. 2003b. *Josephus and the New Testament*. Second edition. Peabody, MA, Hendrickson.

———. 2005a. 'Figured Speech and Irony in T. Flavius Josephus', in Edmondson et al. 2005: 243–88.

———. 2005b. 'Of Audience and Meaning: Reading Josephus' *Bellum Judaicum* in the Context of a Flavian Audience', in Sievers and Lembi 2005: 71–100.

———. 2008. *Flavius Josephus. Translation and Commentary Vol. 1b. Judean War 2*. Leiden, Brill.

———. 2009. 'Of Despots, Diadems and Diadochoi: Josephus and Flavian Politics', in W. J. Dominik, J. Garthwaite, and P. A. Roche (eds.), *Writing Politics in Imperial Rome*. Leiden, Brill: 323–50.

———. 2016a. *A History of the Jewish War*, AD *66–74*. Cambridge, Cambridge University Press.

———. 2016b. 'Josephus' *Autobiography* (*Life of Josephus*)', in Chapman and Rodgers 2016: 59–74.

———. 2016c. 'Josephus' *Judean War*', in Chapman and Rodgers 2016: 13–35.

———. 2019. 'Stranger Danger! Amixia among Judaeans and Others', in G. Van Koonten and J. Van Ruiten (eds.), *Intolerance, Polemics and Debate in Antiquity*. Leiden, Brill: 232–55.

———. 2022. *Flavius Josephus. Translation and Commentary Vol. 2a. Judean War 4*. Leiden, Brill.

McGing, B. and Mossman, J. (eds.) 2006. *The Limits of Ancient Biography*. Swansea, Classical Press of Wales.

McLaren, J. S. 1998. *Turbulent Times? Josephus and Scholarship on Judaea in the First Century* CE. Sheffield, Sheffield Academic Press.

Meyers, E. M. and Chancey, M. A. 2012. *Alexander to Constantine. Archaeology of the Land of the Bible*. New Haven, CT, and London, Yale University Press.

Millar, B. 2000. *The* Siege of Jerusalem *in Its Physical, Literary and Historical Contexts*. Dublin and Portland, OR, Four Courts Press.

Millar, F. 1978. 'The Background to the Maccabean Revolution: Reflections on Martin Hengel's "Judaism and Hellenism"', *Journal of Jewish Studies* 29: 1–21.

Mirguit, F. 2022. 'Josephus's Lamentations in the *Judean War*: Body, Emotional Resistance, and Gender', *JSJ* 53: 524–66.

Misch, G. 1998. *A History of Autobiography in Antiquity*. London, Routledge.
Moehring, H. R. 1984. 'Joseph ben Matthia and Flavius Josephus: The Jewish Prophet and Roman Historian', *ANRW* 2.21.2: 864–944.
Momigliano, A. 1982. 'The Origins of Universal History', in *Annali della Scuola Normale Superiore di Pisa, Classe di Lettere e Filosofia* 3.12.2: 533–60.
Mor, M. and Reiterer, F. V. (eds.) 2010. *Samaritans. Past and Present*. Berlin and New York, De Gruyter.
Nicholson, W. 1919. *The Historical Sources of Defoe's* Journal of the Plague Year. Boston, MA, The Stratford Co.
Nisse, R. 2017. *Jacob's Shipwreck. Diaspora, Translation, and Jewish–Christian Relations in Medieval England*. Ithaca, NY, Cornell University Press.
Noam, V. 2017. 'Lost Historical Traditions between Josephus and the Rabbis', in H. Baden, H. Najman, and E. Tigchelaar (eds.), *Sibyls, Scriptures, and Scrolls. John Collins at Seventy*. Leiden, Brill: 991–1017.
Nodet, E. 1996. *Le Pentateuque de Flavius Josèphe*. Paris, Éditions du Cerf.
Noreña, C. F. 2003. 'Medium and Message in Vespasian's Templum Pacis', *Memoirs of the American Academy in Rome* 48: 25–43.
North, H. F. 1966. 'Canons and Hierarchies of the Cardinal Virtues in Greek and Latin Literature', in L. Wallach (ed.), *The Classical Tradition. Literary and Historical Studies in Honor of Harry Caplan*. Ithaca, NY, Cornell University Press: 165–83.
Noth, M. 1943. *Überlieferungsgeschichtliche Studien. Die sammelnden und bearbeitenden Geschichtswerke im Alten Testament*. Tübingen, Max Niemeyer.
Pagán, V. E. 2005. *Conspiracy Narratives in Roman History*. Austin, TX, University of Texas Press.
Pareles, M. 2023. 'Cannibal Maria in the Siege of Jerusalem: New Approaches', *Religion Compass* 17(12), e12479, https://doi.org/10.1111/rec3.12479.
Parente, F. and Sievers, J. (eds.) 1994. *Josephus and the History of the Greco-Roman Period. Essays in Honor of Morton Smith*. Leiden, New York, and Cologne, Brill.
Pastor, J., Stern, P., and Mor, M. (eds.) 2011. *Flavius Josephus. Interpretation and History*. Leiden and Boston, MA, Brill.
Paul, G. M. 1993. 'The Presentation of Titus in the *Jewish War* of Josephus: Two Aspects', *Phoenix* 47: 56–66.
Pelling, C. B. R. 2006. 'Breaking the Bounds: Writing About Caesar', in McGing and Mossman 2006: 255–80.

———. 2011. 'Velleius and Biography: The Case of Julius Caesar', in E. Cowan (ed.), *Velleius Paterculus. Making History*. Swansea, Classical Press of Wales: 156–76.

Petitfils, J. M. 2014. 'Martial Moses in Flavian Rome: Josephus's *Antiquities* 2–4 and Exemplary Roman Leadership', *Journal of Greco-Roman Christianity and Judaism* 10: 194–208.

Pollard, R. M. 2015. 'The *De Excidio* of "Hegesippus" and the Reception of Josephus in the Early Middle Ages', *Viator* 46(2): 65–100.

Price, J. J. 1992. *Jerusalem under Siege. The Collapse of the Jewish State, 66–70 CE*. Leiden, Brill.

———. 2005. 'The Provincial Historian at Rome', in Sievers and Lembi 2005: 101–18.

———. 2011a. 'Josephus', in A. Feldherr and G. Hardy (eds.), *The Oxford History of Historical Writing Volume 1. Beginnings to AD 600*. Oxford, Oxford University Press: 219–43.

———. 2011b. 'Josephus' Reading of Thucydides: A Test Case', in G. Rechenauer and V. Pothou (eds.), *Thucydides. A Violent Teacher? History and Its Representations*. Göttingen, V&R Unipress: 79–98.

Pucci ben Zeev, M. 1998. *Jewish Rights in the Roman World. The Greek and Roman Documents Quoted by Josephus Flavius*. Tübingen, Mohr Siebeck.

———. 2011. 'Between Fact and Fiction: Josephus' Account of the Destruction of the Temple', in Pastor et al. 2011: 53–63.

Pummer, R. 2009. *The Samaritans in Flavius Josephus*. Tübingen, Mohr Siebeck.

Rad, G. von 1966. 'The Deuteronomistic Theology of History in 1 and 2 Kings', in *The Problem of the Hexateuch and Other Essays*. New York, McGraw-Hill: 205–21.

Rajak, T. 1973. 'Justus of Tiberias', *CQ* 23: 345–68.

———. 1987. 'Josephus and Justus of Tiberias', in L. Feldman and Hata 1987: 81–94.

———. 1998. 'The *Against Apion* and the Continuities in Josephus' Political Thought', in Mason 1998c: 222–46.

———. 2001. *The Jewish Dialogue with Greece and Rome*. Leiden and Boston, MA, Brill.

———. 2002. *Josephus. The Historian and His Society*. Second edition. London, Duckworth.

———. 2009. *Translation and Survival. The Greek Bible of the Ancient Jewish Diaspora*. Oxford, Oxford University Press.

———. 2018. 'The Jewish Diaspora in Greco-Roman Antiquity', *Interpretations* 72: 146–62.

Rapoport, D. C. 1983. 'Fear and Trembling: Terrorism in Three Religious Traditions', in *American Political Science Review* 78: 658–77.

———. 2022. *Waves of Global Terrorism. From 1879 until the Present.* New York, Columbia University Press.

Rappaport, U. 1994. 'Where Was Josephus Lying – in His *Life* or in the *War*?', in Parente and Sievers 1994: 279–89.

———. 2007. 'Josephus' Personality and the Credibility of His Narrative', in Rodgers 2007: 68–81.

Regev, E. 2017. 'The Hellenization of the Hasmoneans Revisited: The Archaeological Evidence', *Advances in Anthropology* 7: 175–96.

Reinhardt, W. 1995. 'The Population Size of Jerusalem and the Numerical Growth of the Jerusalem Church', in R. Bauckham (ed.), *The Book of Acts in Its Palestinian Setting*. Grand Rapids, MI, Eerdmans: 237–65.

Reinhartz, A. 2013. *Caiaphas. The High Priest*. Minneapolis, MN, Fortress Press.

Rengstorf, K. H. 1968–83. *A Complete Concordance to Flavius Josephus*. Leiden, Brill.

Rhoads, D. M. 1976. *Israel in Revolution, 6–74 CE. A Political History Based on the Writings of Josephus*. Philadelphia, PA, Fortress Press.

Richardson, P. and Fisher, A. M. 2017. *Herod. King of the Jews and Friend of the Romans*. Second edition. London and New York, Routledge.

Richmond, I. A. 1962. 'The Roman Siege-Works of Masada, Israel', *JRS* 52: 142–55.

Riggsby, A. M. 2006. *Caesar in Gaul and Rome. War in Words*. Austin, TX, University of Texas Press.

Rodgers, Z. 2006. 'Justice for Justus: A Re-examination of Justus of Tiberias' Role in Josephus' Autobiography', in McGing and Mossman 2006: 169–92.

———. (ed.) 2007. *Making History. Josephus and Historical Method*. Leiden, Brill.

Rogers, G. M. 2021. *For the Freedom of Zion. The Great Revolt of Jews Against Romans, 66–74 CE*. New Haven, CT, Yale University Press.

Roller, D. 1998. *The Building Program of Herod the Great*. Berkeley, CA, University of California Press.

Römer, T. 2020. 'The So-Called Deuteronomistic History and Its Theories of Composition', in B. E. Kelle and B. A. Strawn (eds.), *The Oxford Handbook of the Historical Books of the Hebrew Bible*. Oxford, Oxford University Press: 302–22.

Sanders, E. P. 1992. *Judaism, Practice and Belief, 63 BCE – 66 CE*. Philadelphia, PA, Trinity Press International.

Schäfer, P. 1997. *Judeophobia. Attitudes toward the Jews in the Ancient World*. Cambridge, MA, Harvard University Press.

Schatz, A. (ed.) 2019. *Josephus in Modern Jewish Culture*. Leiden and Boston, MA, Brill.

Schlatter, A. 1923. *Der Bericht über das Ende Jerusalems. Ein Dialog mit Wilhelm Weber*. Gütersloh, Bertelsmann.

Schreckenberg, H. 1972. *Die Flavius-Josephus-Tradition in Antike und Mittelalter*. Leiden, Brill.

———. 1987. 'The Works of Josephus and the Early Christian Church', in L. Feldman and Hata 1987: 315–24.

Schwartz, B., Zerubavel, Y., and Barnett, B. M. 1986. 'The Recovery of Masada: A Study in Collective Memory', *Sociological Quarterly* 27: 147–64.

Schwartz, D. R. 2011. 'Josephus, Catullus, Divine Providence, and the Date of the *Jewish War*', in Pastor et al. 2011: 331–52.

———. 2016. 'Many Sources but a Single Author: Josephus' *Jewish Antiquities*', in Chapman and Rodgers 2016: 36–58.

Schwartz, S. 1986. 'The Composition and Publication of Josephus' *Bellum Iudaicum* Book 7', *HThR* 79: 373–86.

———. 1995. 'Language, Power and Identity in Ancient Palestine', *P&P* 148: 3–47.

———. 2001. *Imperialism and Jewish Society, 200 BCE to 640 CE*. Princeton, NJ, Princeton University Press.

Siegert, F. 2008. *Über die Ursprünglichkeit des Judentums. Contra Apionem*. 2 vols. Göttingen, Vandenhoeck & Ruprecht.

———., Schreckenberg, H., and Vogel, M. (eds. and trans.) 2001. *Flavius Josephus. Aus meinem Leben (Vita)*. Tübingen, Mohr Siebeck.

Sievers, J. and Lembi, G. (eds.) 2005. *Josephus and Jewish History in Flavian Rome and Beyond*. Leiden, Brill.

Smelik, K. A. D. and Hemelrijk, E. A. 1984. '"Who knows not what monsters demented Egypt worships?": Opinions on Egyptian Animal Worship in Antiquity as Part of the Ancient Conception of Egypt', *ANRW* 17.4: 1853–2001.

Smelik, W. F. 2013. *Rabbis, Language and Translation in Late Antiquity*. Cambridge, Cambridge University Press.

Spilsbury, P. 1998. 'God and Israel in Josephus: A Patron–Client Relationship', in Mason 1998c: 172–91.

———. 2002. 'Josephus on the Burning of the Temple, the Flavian Triumph, and the Providence of God', *SBL Seminar Papers* 38: 306–27.

———. 2005. 'Reading the Bible in Rome: Josephus and the Constraints of Empire', in Sievers and Lembi 2005: 209–27.

———. and Seeman, C. 2016. *Flavius Josephus. Translation and Commentary Vol. 6a. Judean Antiquities 11*. Leiden, Brill.

Stanislawski, M. 2004. *Autobiographical Jews. Essays in Jewish Self-Fashioning*. Seattle, WA, University of Washington Press.

Sterling, G. E. 1992. *Historiography and Self-Definition. Josephos, Luke-Acts and Apologetic Historiography*. Leiden, New York, and Cologne, Brill.

———. 2007. 'The Jewish Appropriation of Hellenistic Historiography', in Marincola 2007: 213–24.

Stern, M. 1974–80. *The Greek and Latin Authors on Jews and Judaism*. 3 vols. Jerusalem, Israel Academy of Science and Humanities.

———. 1987. 'Josephus on the Roman Empire as Reflected in the *Jewish War*', in L. Feldman and Hata 1987: 71–80.

Stern, P. 2010. '*Life of Josephus*: The Autobiography of Flavius Josephus', *JSJ* 41: 63–93.

———. 2011. 'Josephus and Justus: The Place of Chapter 65 (336–367) in *Life*, the Autobiography of Flavius Josephus', in Pastor et al. 2011: 381–96.

Stover, J. A. and Woudhuysen, G. 2022. '*Historiarum libri quinque*: Hegesippus between Josephus and Sallust', *Histos* 16: 1–27.

Swift, J. 2018. *Irish Political Writings after 1725*. Edited by D. Hayton and A. Rounce. Cambridge, Cambridge University Press.

Tcherikover, V. 1959. *Hellenistic Civilization and the Jews*. Philadelphia, PA, Jewish Publication Society of America.

Teets, S. C. 2013. '*Charizomenos Herodei*: Josephus' Nicolaus of Damascus in the *Judaean Antiquities*', *Histos* 7: 88–127.

———. 2020. 'The Trauma of Autopsy and the Transgression of History in Josephus' *Jewish War*', *JSJ* 51: 261–84.

Thackeray, H. St-J. 1929. *Josephus. The Man and the Historian*. New York, Jewish Institute of Religion Press.

Thackeray, H. St-J., Marcus, R., Wikgren, A., and Feldman, L. H. (eds.) 1926–65. *Josephus*. Loeb Classical Library. 13 vols. Cambridge, MA, Harvard University Press.

Thérond, B. 1981. 'Les Flaviens dans "La guerre des Juifs" de Flavius Josèphe', *DHA* 7: 235–45.

Toher, M. 1989. 'On the Use of Nicolaus' Historical Fragments', *ClAnt* 8: 159–72.

———. 2003. 'Nicolaus and Herod in the *Antiquitates Judaicae*', *HSPh* 101: 427–47.

Tropper, A. 2005. 'Yohanan ben Zakkai, *Amicus Caesaris*: A Jewish Hero in Rabbinic Eyes', *Jewish Studies Internet Journal* 4: 133–49.

———. 2016. *Rewriting Ancient Jewish History. The History of the Jews in Roman Times and the New Historical Method*. New York and London, Routledge.

———. 2024. '"When I die, kill those elders": The Twice-Told Tale of a Despot's Death', in Czajkowski and Friedman 2024: 58–77.

Van der Horst, P. W. 2002. *Japheth in the Tents of Shem. Studies on Jewish Hellenism in Antiquity*. Leuven, Peeters.

Van Henten, J.-W. 2011. 'Constructing Herod as a Tyrant: Assessing Josephus' Parallel Passages', in Pastor et al. 2011: 193–216.
———. 2013. *Flavius Josephus. Translation and Commentary Vol. 7b. Judean Antiquities 15*. Leiden, Brill.
———. 2015. 'Herod the Great in Josephus', in Chapman and Rodgers 2016: 235–46.
Vandenberghe, M. J. 2016. 'Villains Called Sicarii: A Commonplace for Rhetorical Vituperation in the Texts of Flavius Josephus', *JSJ* 47: 475–507.
Verbrugghe, G. and Wickersham, J. M. 1996. *Berossos and Manetho, Introduced and Translated. Native Traditions in Ancient Mesopotamia and Egypt*. Ann Arbor, MI, University of Michigan Press.
Vidal-Naquet, P. 1977. 'Flavius Josèphe, ou du bon usage de la trahison', in P. Savinel (trans.), *Flavius Josèphe. La guerre des Juifs*. Paris, Éditions de Minuit: 1–117.
———. 1978. 'Flavius Josèphe et Masada', *RH* 260: 3–21.
Vincent, N. 2013. 'William of Newburgh, Josephus, and the New Titus', in S. R. Jones and S. Watson (eds.), *Christians and Jews in Angevin England. The York Massacre of 1190, Narratives and Contexts*. York, York Medieval Press: 57–90.
Vogel, M. 1999. '*Vita* 64–69, das Bilderverbot und die Galiläapolitik des Josephus', *JSJ* 30: 65–79.
Walbank, F. W. 2002. '"Treason" and Roman Domination: Two Case Studies', in *Polybius, Rome and the Hellenistic World*. Cambridge, Cambridge University Press: 258–76.
Walsh, P. G. 1961. *Livy. His Historical Aims and Methods*. Cambridge, Cambridge University Press.
Webster, J. 1995. 'The Just War: Graeco-Roman Texts as Colonial Discourse', in D. Cottam, D. Dungworth, S. Scott, and J. Taylor (eds.), *Proceedings of the Fourth Annual Theoretical Roman Archaeology Conference, Durham, 1994*. Oxford, Oxford University Press: 1–10.
Westwood, U. 2022. 'Prophecies and Princesses: Moses in Egypt and Ethiopia According to Josephus', *Akroterion* 67: 65–84.
———. 2023. *Moses among the Greek Lawgivers: Reading Josephus' Antiquities through Plutarch's Lives*. Leiden and Boston, MA, Brill.
Whealey, A. 2003. *Josephus on Jesus. The Testimonium Flavianum Controversy from Late Antiquity to Modern Times*. New York, Peter Lang.
———. 2016. 'The *Testimonium Flavianum*', in Chapman and Rodgers 2016: 345–55.
Whiston, W. 2006. *The Jewish Antiquities*. Ware, Hertfordshire, Wordsworth Editions.

White, H. 1973. *Metahistory. The Historical Imagination in Nineteenth-Century Europe*. Baltimore, MD, Johns Hopkins University Press.
Wilker, J. 2007. *Für Rom und Jerusalem. Die herodianische Dynastie im 1. Jahrhundert n. Chr.* Frankfurt, Verlag Antike.
Williamson, G. A. 1981. *Josephus. The Jewish War*. Revised by E. M. Smallwood. Harmondsworth, Penguin.
Wiseman, T. P. 2013. *Flavius Josephus. The Death of Caligula*. Liverpool, Liverpool University Press.
Wright, S. K. 1989. *The Vengeance of Our Lord. Medieval Dramatizations of the Destruction of Jerusalem*. Toronto, University of Toronto Press.
Yadin, Y. 1966. *Masada. Herod's Fortress and the Zealots' Last Stand*. Translated by M. Pearlman. London, Weidenfeld and Nicolson.
Yavetz, Z. 1975. 'Reflections on Titus and Josephus', *GRBS* 16: 411–32.

General Index

1 Kings   12
1 Maccabees   16-17, 30, 55
1 Samuel   12

2 Kings   12
2 Maccabees   16-17, 57
2 Samuel   12

Aaron   64-8
Abiram   64-8
Abraham   11, 13, 53, 60
Acts of Peter   103
Adiabene, kingdom of   70
Agrippa II, king   6, 34, 76
Agrippa, M. Vipsanius   68
Agrippina the Younger   75
Albinus, procurator of Judaea   32
Alderman, Naomi   116-7
Alexander the Great   15, 53, 61, 71
Alexander Jannaeus, Hasmonaean dynast   100
Alexandria   7, 9, 93
  Jewish community of   16, 50, 91, 93
Ananus ben Ananus   6, 42
Anilaeus   70
Annas   116-7
Antigonus, Hasmonaean dynast   19
Antiochus III, king   16
Antiochus IV Epiphanes, king   16-17, 24-5
Antipas, heir of Herod   10
Antony   19, 32
Apion 'Pleistonikes'   24-5, 87, 91-5
Apollonius Molon   95-6
apologetics   85-6, 101
Arabic language   104
Aramaic language   8, 16
Archelaus, heir of Herod   20
Aristobulus, Hasmonaean dynast   18-19
Aristotle   22, 45
Artapanus   57
Asinaeus   70
Assyria, Assyrians   13, 52, 71
Augustus, emperor   8, 11, 19, 32, 75
autobiography   *see* biography

Babylon, Babylonians   47, 71
  destruction of First Temple by   13, 45-7
  as analogue of Rome in the works of Josephus   45-7, 53, 59, 71
  as historians of the Jews   89-90
Babylonian Talmud   99-101

bandits and banditry   38-42, 70, 116
Bannus   5
Bede   105
Berossus   54, 57, 60, 89, 118
Beth Horon   6
biography, Greek and Roman   74-6, 83
'biostructuring'   83-4
Britain, Britons
  in the Roman period   6, 34-5
  after the Roman period   106, 109
Byzantine Empire   104

Caesar, C. Julius   19
Caesarea Maritima   11
Caiaphas   116-7
Caligula, emperor   3, 23, 32-3, 55, 69-70, 93
Canaan, Canaanites   11-12, 53
cannibalism   24-5, 46-7, 92, 109
Cassiodorus   87, 104
Cassius, assassin of Caesar   19, 32
Cassius Dio   99
Catullus, governor of Cyrene   50-51
Celsus   23
Cestius Gallus, governor of Syria   26, 34
Chaeremon   90-92
Christians, Christianity   101-6, 108
Christian supersessionism   101-6, 117
Cicero   24, 72
circumcision
  as Jewish custom   17, 24, 94-5
  of Apion 'Pleistonikes'   94-5
Claudius, emperor   70
Clearchus of Soli   22
Cleopatra VII, queen   32
comedy   51, 87
commentarii   30
constitution, Mosaic Law presented as   86-7, 95-8
covenant   11-12, 13, 101
Crassus, M. Licinius   19, 32
crucifixion of Jesus of Nazareth   101-2, 108
Cyrene   8, 50-51
Cyrus the Great, emperor   13

Daniel, Book of   15, 17
Daniel, prophet   53
Dathan   64-8
David, king   12, 13
Davidic dynasty   12
De Excidio Hierosolymitano   103

INDEX

Dead Sea 10, 49
Decapolis 10
Defoe, Daniel 109
deicide, antisemitic accusation of 101-2, 105, 107
Demetrius the Chronographer 57
Destruction de Jérusalem, La 105
Deuteronomistic History 12-13, 26, 46
Deuteronomy, Book of 12, 46
diaspora, Jewish 16
dietary regulations, in Judaism 24
Dio *see* Cassius Dio
Dionysius of Halicarnassus 57-8, 71
Domitian, emperor 8-9, 27, 48, 52-3, 85, 110
dreams as divine visions 6-7, 83

Egypt, Egyptians 10, 15, 104
   and the Exodus 11-12, 22, 23, 63-4, 90-93
   as haters of Jews 91-2
   as historians of the Jews 89-92
   Josephus' mockery of 91-5
Eleazar ben Yair 43, 49-50, 114
emotion in historiography 44-5
English language 105-6, 109
Epaphroditus 9, 53, 72-3, 86, 95
Essenes 5, 97, 99
Esther, Book of 54-5
Eupolemus 57
Eusebius 102
Exodus, Book of 23, 61-3
Ezekiel, Book of 46

Festus, Porcius, procurator of Judaea 32-3
Feuchtwanger, Lion 110-111
Ficino, Marsilio 108
flamen Dialis 14
Flavian dynasty 8-9, 27-28, 34-8, 43, 47-8
Flavius Silva 49-50, 113

Gabinius, Aulus 32-3
Gaius, emperor *see* Caligula
Galilee 6, 10, 12, 27-28, 40, 72-83
Gamala 35
Gaul, Gauls 48
Genesis, Book of 22, 59-60
Germany, Germans
   in the Roman period 34-5
   after the Roman period 110-111
Gessius Florus, Roman procurator of Judaea 6, 26, 32
God *see* Yahweh
'God-fearers' 23
gods 96
Greece, Greeks 16, 18, 88-90, 93
Greek culture and scholarship 18, 60-61, 85, 93
   privileged position under Roman rule 1, 3, 18, 25, 58-9, 60-61, 66-7, 85, 88-90

Greek language 15-16, 58-9
Guttman, Shmaryahu 112

Hardy, Thomas 109
Hasmonaean dynasty 3, 17-18, 26, 53-4
Hata, Prof. Gohei 114-5
Hebrew Bible 11-15, 53-4
Hebrew language 54, 106-7
Hegesippus *see De Excidio Hierosolymitano*
Herod, king 4, 11, 13, 19-20, 26, 30, 32-3, 55, 67-9
Herodian dynasty 20-21, 26, 53-4
Herodotus 24, 61-2, 71, 89, 108
historiography, Greek and Roman 28-9, 44-5, 53-5, 57-8, 62, 71
   Josephus' criticism of 52, 87-90
Hoffman, Alice 115-6
Holy of Holies 14, 18-19
Horace 103
Hyrcanus, Hasmonaean dynast 18-19

Ibn Khaldūn 104
Idumaea, Idumaeans 10, 41
Isaiah, Book of 22-3
Isidore of Seville 105
Isocrates 75
Israel, biblical kingdom 12-13, 53
Israel, modern state 111-4
   Israel Defence Forces (IDF) 112-4
Italy, Italians
   in the Roman period 48
   after the Roman period 106-7, 108

Jacob 11
Japan, Japanese language 114-5
Jason of Cyrene 57
Jeremiah, Book of 46
Jeremiah, prophet 13
Jerusalem 3-4, 6, 10-11, 15, 28, 40-41
   Lower City 4, 42
   Upper City 4, 28, 42, 47
   First Temple of 12, 45-7, 53
   Second Temple of 3-4, 7-8, 13-14, 18-19, 26, 32, 34, 53
   siege and destruction of 7-8, 26, 28, 42, 43-7, 101-6
Jesus ben Gamalas 39-40
Jesus of Nazareth 5, 23, 108
Jewish Revolt (66-73 CE) 5-8, 26-51, 53, 72-84
Jews 9-25
   Greek and Roman attitudes towards 21-5, 85-98
   privileges of under Roman rule 33-4
John of Gischala 40, 41, 47, 74, 80
John Hyrcanus, Hasmonaean dynast 100
Jonathan, refugee *sicarius* 50-51
Jordan, river 10

INDEX

Joseph 11, 60
Josephus
  education of 4-5, 73
  embassy to Nero 5, 73
  family of 3, 9, 29, 73
  command in Galilee 6, 27-28, 72-84
  capture by Vespasian 7
  association with Titus 7-8
  life in Rome 8-9
  as a 'propagandist' 34-8, 43-8
  use of sources 29-30, 54-6
Joshua 12
Jotapata 6, 27-28, 77, 117
Judaea 9-11, 15-16, 18-21, 26-51
Judah, biblical kingdom 10, 12-13, 53
Judaean People's Front, splitters 39
Judaism 14-15, 21-5, 95-8, 99-101, 106-8
Judas the Galilean 33-4
Julius Caesar *see* Caesar, C. Julius
Justus of Tiberias 74, 76-9

Kipling, Rudyard 109
kohanim *see* priests, Jewish
Korah 64-8

Lamdan, Yitzhak 111-2
Lamentations, Book of 46
Latin language 103-4
lepers and leprosy 92
Letter of Aristeas 16, 55
Livy 38, 55, 57, 71, 101, 106
Luke, Gospel of 5
Lysimachus 90-2, 95-6

Maccabean Revolt 16-17, 26, 30-31, 53, 67
Macedon, Macedonians 15-18, 71
Manetho 54, 57, 89, 90-92, 118
Maria of Bethezuba, refugee and cannibal 46-7, 105, 109
Mario, fictional Italian plumber 79
Marius, Gaius 66
Mark Antony *see* Antony
Masada 41-2, 99, 103, 107, 111, 115-6
  Josephus' narrative of the fall of 49-50, 111
  archaeological investigations of 112-3
  receptions of Josephus' narrative of 112-6
Matthew, Gospel of 20
Media, Medes 52, 60, 71
Mishnah 99
Mithridates VI, king 18
Mograbi, Avi 113-4
Moses 11-12, 13, 53, 54-5, 60, 61, 90-93, 95-8
  Greek and Roman knowledge of 22, 23
  as Jewish lawgiver 62, 95-8
  characterization of by Josephus 62-7
myth 60-62, 96

Nabataean kingdom 10
Nazis and Nazism 110-111
Nebuchadnezzar II, king 13, 45-7
Nero, emperor 3, 5, 7, 34, 40, 73
Nerva, emperor 85
Nicolaus of Damascus 30, 55
Noah 62
Numbers, Book of 40, 64-8
Numenius of Apamea 22

O'Toole, Peter 113
Old Testament *see* Hebrew Bible
Olympian Zeus 11, 17
On the Sublime 22
Ovid 24

Palestine, Palestinians 111-4
  British Mandate for Palestine 111-2
Parthia, Parthians 19, 70
pathos *see* emotion in historiography, tragedy
People's Front of Judaea, fictional liberation movement 39
Pericles 42
Persia, Persians 13-15, 30, 53, 60, 71
Pharisees 5, 97, 100, 116-7
  as perceived ancestors of rabbis 117
Philo of Alexandria 11, 118
Philo of Byblos 60, 118
philosophy, Judaism presented as 62, 97-8
Phinehas 40
Phoenicia, Phoenicians 10, 89
Photius 73
Pilate, Pontius, procurator of Judaea 33, 116
Platina, Bartolomeo 108
Plato 22, 89
Pliny the Elder 4, 93, 99
Plutarch 75
Polybius 29, 30, 55
Pompeii 4
Pompey the Great 18-19, 31
Pontius Pilate *see* Pilate, Pontius
Poppaea Sabina 5
Porphyry 99
priests, Jewish 1, 4, 9, 14, 16-17, 21, 34, 40
providence, providential history 26, 36, 42, 45-7, 58-9, 70-71, 82-4
pseudo-Hegesippus *see* *De Excidio Hierosolymitano*
pseudo-Rufinus 104
Ptolemaic dynasty 15-16
Ptolemy II, king 16, 56

Quinctilius Varus *see* Varus, P. Quinctilius
Quintilian 79

rabbinic literature *see* Babylonian Talmud, Mishnah, Tosefta

INDEX

Republic, Roman 18-19, 32, 66
rhetoric 63, 65-8, 80-82, 86
Rome 3, 5, 8, 16, 43, 48, 50-51
Roman Empire 1-2, 20-21, 31-4, 37-8, 47, 53-4, 71, 118-9
Rufinus *see* pseudo-Rufinus

sabbath-observance 15, 24
Sadducees 5, 97, 100
Sallust 103
Salome Alexandra, Hasmonaean queen 18
Samaria, Samaritans 10, 12
sanhedrin 21
Saul, king 12
Sea of Galilee 10
Sefer Yosippon 104, 106-7, 111
Seleucid dynasty 15, 16-18, 30-31
Senate, Roman 19
Sepphoris 10
Septuagint bible 16, 54, 56
Sibylline Oracles 61
sicarii (*see also* Masada) 40-41, 49-50, 113, 115-6
Siege of Jerusalem, The 105-6
Silius Italicus 49
Simon bar Gioras 41-2, 47
slavery, as metaphor for colonial rule 31, 37-8
Slavonic Josephus 104
Solomon, king 12
stasis 27-8, 38-9, 48, 64-8, 80
  in Thucydides 38-9
  among Jewish rebel factions 27-28, 38-9, 50
  among Romans (69 CE) 7, 27-8
Strabo 22, 30, 55
Suetonius 37, 75, 99
Suetonius Paulinus 75
suicide 7, 49-50, 106-7, 111-3
Sulla, L. Cornelius 75, 83
succession of empires *see translatio imperii*
supersessionism *see* Christian supersessionism
Swift, Jonathan 109
symphonia 88-9, 92, 96-8
Syria 10, 18, 21, 34

Tacitus 4, 22, 23-4, 70, 75-6, 81, 99, 103, 118
Talmud *see* Babylonian Talmud
Tanakh *see* Hebrew Bible
Tarichaeae 35-6, 82
taxation, Roman 33-4
Temple of Jerusalem *see* Jerusalem, First Temple of; Jerusalem, Second Temple of
Tertullian 86
Testimonium Flavianum 108
theocracy 98

Thucydides 8, 26, 28-29, 42, 45, 52, 54, 64-5, 108
Tiberias 10, 77-8
Tiberius, emperor 93
Tiberius Julius Alexander, Roman administrator 33, 110
Titus, general and emperor 6-9, 26, 27-28, 48, 104, 110
  Josephus' characterization of 36-7
  clemency of 36-7
  responsibility for destruction of Jerusalem Temple 37, 43-7
Torah, Torah-observance 5, 9, 14-15, 40, 53, 59, 82, 117
Tosefta 99
tradition, traditionalism
  Jewish 33-4
  Roman 5, 33-4, 87
  opposed to Greek innovation 96-7
tragedy 44-5, 51, 69
Trajan, emperor 85, 110-111
Transjordan 10, 46
translatio imperii 71
triumph of Vespasian and Titus (71 CE) 8, 48, 103
Twain, Mark 109
tyrants and tyranny 39, 64-6, 69

Ur of the Chaldees 11

Varro 23
Varus, P. Quinctilius 33
Vespasian, general and emperor 6-9, 26, 27-8, 48, 73-4, 100, 104
  Josephus' characterization of 34-6
  participation in Roman civil war of 69 CE 7, 27-28, 36, 48, 105
Vindicta Salvatoris 105-6
Virgil 22-3, 103, 106

Whiston, William 109
William of Malmesbury 105
William of Newburgh 106
Wissenschaft des Judentums 107

Xenophon 75

Yadin, Prof. Yigael 112-3
Yahweh 4, 11-15, 31, 36, 45-7, 49-51, 64-8, 70-71, 82-3, 101-6, 110
Yavneh 100
Yiddish language 107
Yohanan ben Zakkai 100-101
Yom Tov 106
York, mass suicide of Jewish community of (1190) 106

zealots 39-40, 113, 114